BREAKING UP, BREAKING DOWN,

&

BREAKING THROUGH

BREAKING UP, BREAKING DOWN, & BREAKING THROUGH

Growing from Pain to Gain

Susan Truett Trammell

TABLE OF CONTENTS

BREAKING UP, BREAKING DOWN, & BREAKING THROUGH

■ ■ ■

Break-ups, and their resulting redefinition of our lives, are a natural part of our humanity. A loss or an ending often involves a crisis. When something bad happens, we have three choices: we can let it define us, let it destroy us, or let it strengthen us. This book focuses on the ways losses of many different sorts can empower us to learn and grow, and in doing so, to live the life we've come to live.

Typical of our Western culture, we tend to either understate or overstate the importance of endings. Whether the loss is the death of a loved one or a job termination, we're often told to "be strong," "what doesn't kill you makes you stronger," and other declarations that tend to dismiss or belittle the impact of significant separations.

In the process of disengaging from someone or something that has held an important place in our hearts and lives, the landscapes of our lives change in significant ways. The former contexts in and through which we've known ourselves are dismantled, and many of the habits, behaviors, and practices that once defined us no longer are relevant. A separation can happen in a moment, but the process that begins with an ending may take years. Our sense of identity may change in significant ways and may occur over time. The more we've invested in a person or activity that is now gone, the greater our sense that we've lost a part of ourselves as well.

As we learn to release the investment we've had in something or someone outside of ourselves, we can open to actually becoming more of who we truly are. What was once is now gone; what is yet to be is beginning. But before our new beginning becomes clear, we may go through a time of disorientation, or as some call this period, the void or a wilderness experience. This is often a time when our faith becomes extremely important to us, and yet we may feel separated from all that very faith has meant. When that happens we may collapse, literally or figuratively, into a mess, an unrecognizable shadow of our former self.

Yet as frightening as this time of transition feels, this is our opportunity to shape a new purpose and identity for ourselves. Just as a tree needs the cold of winter to prepare for spring, so we need this period in the void to prepare for our new life. And as T.S. Eliot describes this time in his *Four Quartets*, "*To arrive where you are, to get from where you are not, you must go by a way wherein there is no ecstasy.*"

In this tumultuous time we struggle with feelings such as fear, anger, confusion, perhaps guilt or remorse, and ultimately grief. At other times we feel empty, cold, flat, a mere outline of who we once were. These are feelings we can't just "snap out of." It's impossible, or so it seems, to pick ourselves up and get back on the track we once knew as life. We're challenged to draw on our deepest inner resources, and indeed as we do, we begin to birth something larger that sees beyond the limitations of our former self.

Let's together examine how like the proverbial Phoenix we can shake off our ashes, move beyond our difficulties, and discover a new orientation and way of being in the world. Ultimately the only REAL loss we suffer is our unwillingness to engage life, recognizing that constant change and growth are what we're being called to accept in order to heal and discover a greater sense of wholeness. Have you ever seen the bumper sticker that declares, "sh_t happens?" It does indeed. But rather than dwelling in the "sh_t" and letting it stop us, loss invites us to choose how we deal with what has happened. Choice is our ultimate power, and we choose every minute of every day. You came into this life to realize and express that very power, which is your essence. And as we encounter changes – some incvitable, others not – who we THINK we are can grow into to who we KNOW we are, as pain opens us to understanding a new and higher way to live.

When something hurts, we learn how to embrace whatever is happening as a source for strength. We learn to be brave and fully alive even during the darkest hours. Everything that occurs becomes a teacher, a source of wisdom. When we live with loving kindness toward every moment, as it happens, we eventually move from baby steps to quantum leaps along our spiritual path, relating to our circumstances with an open heart rather than one blocked by fear and suffering and closed to possibilities. At all times simply remember than nothing happens *TO* us, it all happens *FOR* us – to learn from, grow from, and move ahead from. That's the path that leads you to not just surviving the difficult times, but thriving from all the opportunities they present.

Part I
Breaking Up

1

WHEN LOVE GOES SOUTH

■ ■ ■

As the song says, and as most of us can attest, breaking up *is* hard to do! When I use that term - breaking up - I'm referring to more than just divorce or the end of a love affair. I'm also talking about losses such as the death of a dear one, job separation (by choice or otherwise), loss of a pet or other cherished companion, a dream that now seems beyond our grasp, and any other occurrence that invites grief into our hearts. And some of these situations certainly feel more catastrophic than others.

In our Western culture we've failed in many ways to honor loss, especially when defined as death, in truly healthy ways. And that's basically because most of us are uncomfortable around death, even discussing the idea. We celebrate beginnings, but we typically lament endings. We rejoice at a birth, while we see death as tragic. Marriage is an occasion for celebration; divorce tends to be viewed as unpleasant, even distasteful. And for some, divorce is something to be avoided at all costs.

Now in my sixties as I am writing this book, I've personally experienced just about every kind of break-up imaginable. And I've not only survived, but sooner or later these experiences have created opportunities for me to thrive. There's no denying: loss is tough and requires time in order to heal at the depth that invites a healthy future. Yet breaking up is one of this life's essential growth processes. And while as humans pain is part of our process, suffering is optional. That speaks to the relative brevity of the breaking-up period.

While I agree that time helps the healing process, other ingredients can certainly bring us comfort and aide with the hurt and loss we're feeling. As is the case with all the "breaks" this book addresses, each one offers a challenge that encourages transformation. All, or at least most, are occasions for grief, although a sense of relief sometimes may accompany the sadness.

We grieve when we lose something or someone we have loved; and the transient nature of life makes love and loss intimate companions. That means that in the face of a break-up or loss, we must learn to continue to love. In doing so, we will awaken to even more profound connections. Any time we feel pain, we must learn ways to heal so that we restore emotional well-being and balance. Because loss often brings up fear, we need to understand this other very human feeling and how to turn it into something of benefit.

Think about FEAR for a moment. What is it that you're afraid of, and why? Fear is a common reaction to growth and change, especially as we move forward to someplace we've never been before. Most often our fear is born from past limited beliefs about what is possible. Our fears may be knee-jerk reactions to old programming. But rather than seeing fear as a stop-sign, we can learn to appreciate it as a line that delineates the old from the new. Fears are, in fact, signs of growth. We can embrace our fears rather than hiding or running away from them. We fear death and change of any sort. The unknown is scary. And while in one sense loss is permanent, what is NOT lost is the possibility for new beginnings.

Before I go further, let me encourage you to NEVER think of yourself as a *loser*! Just because you've lost something important in your life does NOT turn you into a loser. Your life itself is a series of endings and beginnings. As we come to the end of anything – a job, an interest, a relationship – we simultaneously find ourselves at a new beginning. And while in the earliest moments and days of any loss, we tend to focus on what is now absent, we also find ourselves becoming a new someone, a person who is now defined differently. You're no longer married, now you're a single person; you're no longer employed, you're now a job seeker; you're an empty-nester now that your children have all grown and moved on. And the definitions that constitute such changes, or new beginnings, are countless.

At the most elemental level of our being, each breath we exhale is a death, as each new inhalation is born. Life goes on and as it does each transition offers an opportunity to start something new. In **The Lion King**, Elton John's words to *The Circle of Life* impart this very message:

From the day we arrive on the planet
And blinking, step into the sun
There's more to see than can ever be seen
More to do than can ever be done

. . . .

It's the Circle of Life
And it moves us all
Through despair and hope
Through faith and love
Till we find our place
On the path unwinding
In the Circle
The Circle of Life

Wherever we are on this circle of Life, we're exactly where we need to be in order to learn what we're here to discover, and grow in the ways we're designed to develop. The greater the challenge, the grander the potential. The rhythm of life into which we've all been born constantly creates for us opportunities to "let go." And when we resist in an effort to hold on – to what was, a memory, a loss – we become disconnected from this ebb and flow of life all around us. When that happens, our will to move on, our choice to make the best of what has changed, is always up to us and to our ability to shine a light on any apparent darkness.

A dear friend, lyricist, and singer calls his latest CD *The Art of Living*. There **IS** an art to living. And we each create our lives with our choices. Each thought is a brush stroke that in some way defines us at that moment. If we choose to stay attached to our pain, our loss and fears, we breathe into emptiness. If we choose to love more deeply what remains, most notably ourselves, then we breathe into the fullness of Life. When we continue to love in the face of loss, we begin the healing process and allow it to teach us that the good, the beauty, the love of *what was* will always remain a part of us. Life continues even when we can no longer see it or touch it or experience it on this sensory plane. We can remember, while not continuing to live in the past. Our challenge is to continue living and loving in ways that give new form to what we once knew. And in that process, rather than becoming something *less*, we become something *greater*. As we do, a new self is born. We BREAK OPEN a new self, one that moves us along our path to our greatest yet to be!

Throughout this book when the time calls it forth, I will remind you of what Kahlil Gibran says about PAIN in his seminal work, **The Prophet**:

Your pain is the breaking of the shell that encloses your understanding.
Even as the stone of the fruit must break,
That its heart may stand in the sun,
So must you know pain.
And could you keep your heart in wonder
At the daily miracles of your life,
Your pain would not seem less wondrous than your joy;
And you would accept the seasons of your heart
Even as you have always accepted the seasons that pass over your fields.
And you would watch with serenity
Through the winters of your grief.
Much of your pain is self-chosen.
It is the bitter potion by which the physician within you
Heals your sick self.
Therefore trust the physician,
And drink his remedy in silence and tranquility.

We can never move ahead as long as we live in the past. But as we ⌐ the best that we once had before the break-up and allow that positive energy to enliven us as it will do, we invite into our lives new relationships and experiences that will both teach us and allow us to help others grow and heal.

As I write these pages I am in the midst of a break-up with my partner. If you've read my earlier title, *Outrageous Loving!*, you have met this man I call Mr. Right. We've lived together for almost a year now, an intimate relationship that has taught me much, much about myself. This isn't my first break-up from a loving relationship. The one constant through them all is what great teachers each and every man has been for me. And more good news: with each subsequent dissolution of a relationship, the painful parting process has lasted a shorter time than ever before. That is, I have moved through it more quickly, more smoothly, and with ever greater insights. This is the beauty of what happens when we connect with Spirit and invite wounds to heal in the presence of increased love and understanding.

The reason for our break-up is what lawyers call "irreconcilable differences." I think of it as misunderstandings. What was true for us both is that words and actions were often misinterpreted or not understood as they were intended. It's difficult at best, and for us impossible, to establish and maintain a truly intimate alliance in the presence of the fall-out from such situations. Obstinacy, on both our parts, did nothing to placate the matter. Anger and frustration were the immediate reactions when such disputes occurred. And with what would prove the final straw, the one that broke the proverbial camel's back, an unwillingness to communicate added fuel to the flames. And we both knew better!

Our differences resulted at least in part from our very contrasting backgrounds - our previous experiences and relationships that led to the way we react, respond, and feel when something occurs. What we've experienced in the past is a mighty influence on how we react in the present. And when those experiences have been negative ones, until we release the memories from our minds and hearts, we will continue to expect the worst. Wouldn't it be more pleasant to anticipate the best?

That's what we need to learn to do. I hope I can help you do just that, so the disappointments of the past are no longer prologue.

As fast and furiously as the final fire erupted between Mr. R and me, within forty-eight hours (and two sleepless nights!) I came out unscathed on the other side. I believe my process is worth sharing, not only because the pain did not become suffering, but even more important, because the dawn that followed the darkness was as bright as any I've ever experienced. I felt at peace, in balance, and very clear about what was mine to do. And what that was primarily was to mend a "broken heart" as quickly as possible. That process begins when we recognize the benefits we've gained from a relationship break-up and invite them to move us forward along our path. At the same time I could give thanks for all the good times we'd experienced. And we must surrender into peace. Resistance makes moving forward impossible.

While to most of our friends, families, and acquaintances, our relationship was difficult to understand, Mr. R and I knew we had reconnected as and when we did quite intentionally. We were, in fact, picking up where we'd left off in an earlier association, and in an earlier lifetime. Whether or not you believe in, or at least understand, the concept of reincarnation, it is a familiar one to both of us. As such, even amid our surprise at reuniting as we did, we never questioned why our reunion had occurred. There remained "work" for us to do as a couple, however that might unfold, and however our past lives together had been intertwined.

Mr. R is a spiritual teacher and highly evolved individual. When we first met I anticipated our working together, delivering seminars, workshops, and classes focused on helping others achieve their life's greatest potential. I also looked forward to shaping a committed intimate relationship with a man I greatly admired and knew I could love. An author, speaker, and singer/song-writer, Mr. R is accomplished in many other surprising (to me) and unrelated fields. Early on I could see that anything he did, he did to the highest possible standards – which he achieved, if not effortlessly, certainly with tenacity and vision. And the knowing that he could accomplish whatever he turned his mind toward.

As I re-examine how our relationship unfolded, its peaks as well as its valleys, I can see a pattern in the lessons that were present along the way. I was certainly not one of Mr. R's creations, and early on he told me he was not in my life as a teacher. But it didn't take long for me to discover how mistaken he was in that regard!

In all my relationships, whatever their duration or nature, I've always believed that for two individuals to achieve and maintain any degree of intimacy and real meaning in their togetherness, they both will have something to learn and something to teach the other. When that no longer is the case, the relationship in all likelihood will end. Such was the case when I'd been married to my husband for forty years, and such occurred after as short a time as six months in a later committed bond. So duration is irrelevant, while content or meaningfulness is all-important.

Each of our "takes" on another – person or situation – is born of our experiences, our biases and prejudices, and our perspective. And while no one knows us better than we do, we can learn a lot about another through the nature of our relationship. But again, what we believe belongs to us. And as Don Miguel Ruiz tells us in *The Four Agreements*, what someone else thinks or says about another is their "garbage" – don't take it personally! Nothing another does is because of us: it's because of themselves. Whenever we eat their emotional garbage, it becomes our own. Not something we want! Trust yourself, never another.

My break-up with Mr. R followed a short yet intense time living together. My break-up eight years earlier from my husband was a very different experience. It actually took us five and a half years to finalize our divorce, meaning we were married forty-five plus years! That's quite an accomplishment; and no one can ever accuse me of being commitment phobic.

In my opinion, based on my personal experiences and those of friends, living under the same roof twenty-four/seven is the best, possibly only, way to really get to know someone, to discover if you're compatible as a couple. Weekends together and trips can certainly tell you some things about another; but until you start co-habitating, particularly in an intimate way if that's the nature of the relationship, you don't really have opportunities to see that person's warts and dark-side, however you may view that individual absent your rose-colored glasses.

Wearing those rose-colored glasses is what happens during that wonderful, romantic "falling in love" period, when both parties typically are not only on their best behavior, but are behaving in the manner they believe will best satisfy their partner's expectations and desires. It's a lovely but certainly unrealistic time of life; and unfortunately for many, it leads directly into marriage or a similar period of commitment.

It didn't take Mr. R and me very long at all, perhaps a week as I recall, before we had the gloves off (as well as the glasses!) and were engaging in our first of what would be many verbal battles. While I'm comfortable with verbal jousting, I was neither familiar nor comfortable with what I think of as verbal abuse. My long-term marriage had always been very civilized; yes, we argued, but did so in a very low-keyed way. So when Mr. R blew his stack, as I perceived his reaction to something I innocently triggered, I was totally caught off-guard. Frankly, his temper frightened me. I never got used to it, and even its final outburst was scary.

I know other couples, most notably my sister and her husband of nearly fifty years, who raise their voices (yell!) at one another, as if there's nothing more natural, when they disagree about something. But that's not the case for me, and to this day I'm uncomfortable with what I consider hurtful displays of temper. Maybe that's because I don't react in kind. So when Mr. R lost his temper "at" me, his voice and words DID hurt.

I expressed my concern with this behavior, but unfortunately his temper flare-ups continued. When I decided I'd had enough of our communication *mis*-communications, we agreed it was time to split. Their provocation was certainly significant, another reason we didn't stay the course.

The primary reason for our break-up involved one of the three key ingredients any couple needs in order for their relationship to be healthy and happy. Those three are effective communication (our primary issue), shared commitment, and a willingness to compromise (a secondary issue for us). Unfortunately for two individuals who both pride themselves on their expert communication skills, we failed miserably in our personal one-on-one exchanges!

When author Gary Chapman talks about the "five love languages" (***The 5 Love Languages: The Secret to Love That Lasts***, Northfield Publishing, 2015), he stresses that compatibility depends on each partner's understanding and applying his or her mate's primary love language in order for a committed relationship to last. When I read Chapman's book, I recognized my primary love language as physical touch; but almost as important for me is the language of communication, which he labels "words of affirmation." Mr. R's primary relationship language *IS* communication. Chapman points out that while kind words are the way these "communication-minded" individuals most feel loved, when unkind words are slung their way, watch out!

While the past cannot be erased, it *can* be forgiven and released. Never bring failures forward; that only leads to resentment and further regret. We choose with every thought we think and word we speak. Sincere apology and sincere attempts to "do better" wherever we may have fallen short can re-glue what may be undermining a relationship. But as is always the case with a couple, it takes two. Both parties must be willing to commit to understanding their partner better and being more sensitive to what works and what doesn't for that individual.

More about how communication skills affect a relationship. Perhaps one of you is a talker, while the other prefers a contemplative existence. Can two such different needs co-exist in a compatible manner? I suggest that yes, they can, given some additional considerations. A friend once asked me this question: since we know your partner can never be the answer to all your wants and needs, can the ones that individual is missing be met in some other way? In other words, if, for example, I enjoy reading and discussing the books I read, can I find a book club to explore and satisfy that need? A tougher one: if I'm a snuggler (which I am), and my partner doesn't like touching (or being touched), can I find a substitute snuggler to meet my need? Hmmmm... Will my furry friend do; or how about self-touch? Maybe a regular trip to my masseuse. Or is this need a deal-breaker when my partner can't or won't reciprocate, and can't or won't learn to enjoy my touch?

Chapman's suggestion about discovering and responding to your partner's love language certainly has merit. Learning to express and receive love "sympathetically" (my descriptor) can definitely enhance an intimate relationship.

2

A LONG JOURNEY ENDS

■ ■ ■

While Mr. R and I agreed when it was time to end our relationship, when my marriage of forty years came to an end, it was a very different and much more difficult time for both parties. Married at twenty, when he was twenty-three, we had dated seriously for the previous three years. So not only did we have a pretty good handle on what the other person was like, we also both knew each other's family and history. He and I basically grew up into adulthood together, a VERY different experience from meeting someone when we were in our sixties. I hate to say I, or anyone else, is set in our ways. But with six decades of experience behind me, and the same for Mr. R, we had established ways of *doing life*," as well as ingrained habits of all kinds that make such a later-in-life romance especially challenging. At least that was my case.

As I've looked back on my married life with a man I've never stopped loving, I can appreciate how growing up together allowed us to know our partner intimately and to play off that person, as each of us shaped our preferences, tastes, habits, and ways of doing and being as we matured. Our economic, social, and educational backgrounds were very similar. We were still forming what I'll call our philosophies of life, or defining for ourselves a spiritual core belief system.

Our son, and our only child, was born after we'd been married for sixteen years. Obviously we'd had all that prior time to really get to know one another. For much of that period, one or the other of us had been in school while working, I earning my MBA, followed by his getting a law degree. When first married we had left our home town and families in Atlanta, moving to Washington, D.C., where – at the height of the Viet Nam war – he was commissioned in the United States Coast Guard. We so enjoyed our time in D.C. that we remained there in our respective corporate positions for fifteen years. Those were great years, both of us active in our careers and busy social life.

When we returned home to Atlanta and our son was born, by choice my life changed and I became a full-time mother. Until he left for college, our son became the focus of our marriage for his first eighteen years. In a somewhat stereotypical manner, when we became empty-nesters, my husband and I began growing apart. By then we were both in our fifties. Over the following five years I increasingly felt that we were no longer teaching or learning from one another. In fact our personal and work interests had diverged to the point that we seemed to no longer understand or be particularly interested in what the other was doing. My attention had turned to ministry, while his continued to progress in his chosen field of architecture. Our single shared interest had become our dogs; but even taking our greyhound to coursing events where he could race as an amateur held insufficient appeal. Instead of having other couples as shared friends, as we'd enjoyed in earlier times, now we each seemed to have our own individual friends and rarely went out together socially. In the rather strange manner I behaved, as I've described in my earlier book, *The Sacred Alchemy of Love*, I was the one to cause our break-up. So what exactly happened, and why, after many good to great years of marriage?

My non-sexual love affair with a man I later discovered was gay led me to file for divorce on the grounds of irreconcilable differences. Our split was acrimonious, to say the least. Not only did I lose my spouse, I lost my home and a very significant financial base. Fortunately, by that time our son was grown, out of college and beginning his professional life in his own home. For that we were both thankful.

14

After both of us had spent more money than we cared to remember on lawyers who ultimately were unable to help us finalize our divorce, following that first year apart, we decided we could work out the terms ourselves. Ultimately we did, but it took both a "time-out," which allowed us each to become more balanced in our relationship, as well as several additional years before we finalized terms. During almost that entire five-year-plus period, each of us had met someone. The man I became involved with was my transitional guy, a man who also was instrumental in saving my life. We remain close friends to this day. My husband had met the woman he would marry two years after our divorce.

Many of you, especially anyone who's been in a long-term marriage such as ours, may ask why, after so many years together, we didn't just hang in there. After all, who wants to risk "everything," plus have to start over in the relationship department? Friends of mine frequently told me how "courageous" I was. When driven by fear I sought to reconcile, my ex, fortunately, had the wisdom to say no. A few months before we'd separated we'd *had* (not celebrated) our fortieth anniversary. I had spent the day in tears, asking myself over and over again, was our marriage worth saving. We both knew it had become something far less than we desired it to be. That evening I asked my husband what his principle reason for staying with me was. His reply, emotional support. When asked the same question, I replied, financial support. How stereotypical our answers were! Had ours become simply a marriage of convenience? It's certainly EASIER to stay together than split. But what is the price you pay if you remain in a lifeless marriage?

As I explain in **Outrageous Loving!**, I knew I needed to grow more; and the confines of our marriage had become suffocating. My ex's first love, then and now, has always been his work. And how many people are fortunate enough to be able to say they truly love the work they do! So as he dug ever more deeply into that source of satisfaction, I literally moved on and began new adventures. I was choosing to honor the sanctity of my individuality in order to evolve. Yes, I was responsible for setting the wheels in motion that led to our divorce; but at the same time, and due to the unusual nature of my "affair," something even more powerful within me was at work. Had I not left that all-too-safe marriage, I probably would never have become a published author, recognized speaker, or learned the many new lessons that I needed to master in this lifetime.

Our marital break-up was the result of both a failure to communicate and our inability and unwillingness to WORK at keeping our marriage vibrant. Our conversations had become increasingly brief; and unfortunately, at that time neither of us knew about love languages or other tools to reignite a spark that was barely flickering.

ANY relationship - an intimate one, a professional one, a familial one, or just a friendship – takes work to maintain, and a great deal of work to improve. A successful and rewarding pay-off typically results. But how many of us are willing to expend time and energy on our relationships? Yet isn't it a shame when we don't – or much more than just a shame? Treasure the effort you put into any relationship worth maintaining. It's been my experience that when I extend myself, the other party is very likely to reciprocate and a steady bond can be established. I love to hear about friends who have kept up with each other since childhood or high school, or some other early period. Unfortunately, I have not fared so well. And that's no one's choice but my own.

To use a gardening metaphor, we sometimes just outgrow the pot we're in. For instance, I had become pot-bound and eventually would have died had I not moved out of my marriage. Yes, I was safe; but I wasn't being and doing what I needed to in order to grow and flourish. I was crying to myself to be placed in a larger container so that my life could continue to evolve. Being pot-bound was okay for a while; it invited me to grow new shoots and begin expressing in new ways. But eventually parts of me would have started to die off; so I needed to transplant myself in a larger container, one that was outside my marriage pot. I was ready to grow into something greater than I had become.

In any relationship there will be plenty of times when individuals disappoint us and circumstances seem to erode our foundation. Other people don't behave according to my desires and designs, and I must realize and accept that fact. When something is over, it's over. Why waste energy on regret, blame, or "it might have been?" With a little, or a lot, of time, clarity and understanding of why a relationship break-up occurred may come; or it may not. The wisest and best choice is to move on. Reflect. Let go. If we insist on resisting a change when it's called for, we do ourselves great harm. In addition to wasting energy and causing ourselves to suffer (our choice!), we are unable to welcome something new and healthier into our lives. When we resist, pain persists. Letting go and surrendering to something greater will be our salvation when break-ups occur. And they will.

Can break-up's be mended, once they've occurred? Sometimes, certainly. Years after our separation, I asked myself (more than once) if my marriage could have not only been saved, but resuscitated. Could I have found ways to achieve what I needed, what was missing for me at that time? Perhaps, certainly in some ways; but I believe certain needs could never have been met if I'd remained a married woman.

How hard did either my spouse or I want to work in order to hold our marriage together? We never found out, because we never discussed the matter. His anger at me, he ultimately admitted, had been growing over many years because of a much earlier issue we'd never discussed in ways that would have enabled him to release his resentment toward me. Carrying such baggage forward sooner or later will result in a break-up, if not a break-down. As challenging as it may be to bring annoyances into the light of day so they can be discussed and fuel growth, the effort typically proves itself worthwhile with the greater intimacy and openness a couple will gain in the process of discovery.

The longer we hold on to grievances, resentments, or any negative feelings, the heavier our baggage becomes. Ultimately it will, in some manner or other, break our backs! In our marriage I, admittedly, had carried the majority of my husband's emotional baggage. In the earliest days of our separation, I felt exuberantly, indescribably free. I remember dancing around the home where I was staying, arms out flung and feeling energized in ways I'd seldom experienced. I had put down all the baggage I'd been carrying for him over many years. It was one of the most exhilarating periods of my life.

3

DEATH OF A BELOVED

■ ■ ■

We've all lost someone for whom we deeply cared through death. Western society prefers to mourn rather than celebrate death as many other societies do. Such celebration is becoming more commonplace in our country as families are choosing to recognize all the ways in which an individual has blessed their lives and this planet. But grieving is necessary and important; it is love's healing work for loss. It can be an honoring and life-affirming activity that offers us comfort in the midst of challenge.

Whether we celebrate a life that once was or mourn its loss in our life, a loved one's passing offers us an incredible opportunity for exploration and growth. While the valley of the shadow of death is long and dark indeed, the time we spend passing through it invites us to explore the mysteries of both life and love. Knowing that nothing we've once loved is never lost brings great comfort during such a time. Opening to the unknown rather than shutting down out of fear is the path to engaging life at ever deeper levels than we have previously.

Someone once said that suffering increases when we want life to be other than it is. Touché! An even more familiar saying, attributed to Aldous Huxley, is that experience is not what happens to you, but how you respond to what happens. Since we know that any ending is accompanied by a new beginning, how can we make ourselves available to all that loss of a beloved to death invites?

Let's explore some of the most common emotions that accompany a loss to death. Those include, but are not limited to, fear, the feeling of being alone, a sense that an underpinning of your own foundation exists no longer, and confusion about your place in the world, now that a special relationship has been severed. Other emotions, depending on the circumstances surrounding the death, might include regret, guilt, blame, and perhaps even a sense that you're being punished. And of course, through all of these experiences, we feel pain. Whatever the discomfort, focusing on the past, what is no longer in your life as opposed to what IS present, keeps one caught in a cycle of fear and despair. The only way to escape those negative and destructive feelings is to face them and move through them. Denial only makes the situation worse; and turning those emotions into anger or blame exacerbates the situation even more.

I want to share a personal case of denial that involved my beloved father's passing from complications following successful surgery to remove a cancerous lung. As is far too common these days, he was released from the hospital too soon. The result was an intestinal blockage of such magnitude that emergency treatment couldn't save his life. While he lingered in the ICU, our immediate family gathered to comfort him, and each other. The original surgeon was at a loss: the lung surgery had gone exceptionally well; there was no reason for impending death. But of course there was, and we knew exactly what had happened. My dad, always the ultimate pragmatist, requested a morphine drip. We were surprised when the doctor in charge consented. We three children totally supported our father's request and understood his desire to not linger in pain. Our mother, understandably, wanted to hold out for what could only be called a miracle.

When the morphine injection was delivered, we asked the doctor how long Dad might linger. We were told it could be as long as several weeks since his overall health was very good. Dad died within twenty-four hours. Clearly his soul was ready to move on and his body simply followed.

Before he was released after his lung surgery, I spent several days with Dad in his recovery room. We were of like minds when it came to our life's philosophy and fundamental belief system. I read to him from Eric Butterworth's **Discover the Power within You**. In earlier years Dad had shared with me William James' **Varieties of Religious Experience**. We knew we shared similar spiritual viewpoints. During my visits Dad explained, and not for the first time, how he never wanted to be a burden on his family. He had often said that when the time came, he would find a way to leave this earth's plane. And so he would.

When his death arrived, the greatest emotion I experienced was that of gratitude: gratitude for this passing which we both knew meant that I, as the only local child, would need to look after our mother rather than care-take for TWO declining parents. Yes, I certainly was sad, as I'd lost my dearest friend who understood me better than even my husband. But I didn't grieve Dad's loss, at least not at that time.

About nine months later my beloved greyhound, Orlando's Racer, died. Although he had outlived the loss of a leg due to osteosarcoma some four years earlier, his death resulted from his organs naturally shutting down at his ripe-old age of thirteen. The grief I experienced with Racer's passing went way beyond what any pet, no matter how beloved, warranted. And the pain went on and on. Finally I recognized that I was grieving for Racer's passing, yes, but more importantly, for my dad's passing months earlier. At that time I had become so involved in my mother's care that I didn't allow myself to feel my most deeply held emotion, that of sadness. So the grief finally came out and with it an even greater appreciation for all my dad's life had meant to me. That release eventually allowed me to grow up in unexpected ways. Any suppressed grief due to loss will ultimately come flowing out, adding to the present moment's pain. And that combination of losses can be overwhelming.

Can you remember the very first death of a loved one? For me it was my beloved grandfather's death when I was just fourteen. He had been my dad's substitute the first five years of my life, when Dad was hospitalized in the tuberculosis sanitarium where no contact was permitted. While my mother had to go to work to support my sister and me, my care was largely left to my maternal grandparents.

My Irish Protestant grandmother was a tough lady, in her mid-sixties when I was more or less dropped in her lap. She demonstrated her love in ways that I later realized was born from fear. My grandfather, however, was the person I always associated with heart-felt loving and tenderness. I clearly remember the cold, snowy day of his funeral. Mom, Dad, my siblings and I had driven to Rhode Island from Alabama in near blizzard conditions. Grandpa had died peacefully in his sleep when his heart simply stopped. His was the gentle kind of passing most of us would like. His casket was open and I recall how horribly difficult it was for me to gaze on his loving face which no longer smiled back at me as he always had. When I returned to my seat, in the front row with other family members, I was seated next to my grandmother. I was wearing a green velvet suit my mother had made, my favorite Sunday clothes. As I sat in respect and grief, Grandma started pulling my skirt down, attempting to cover my knees. She clearly found the sight undignified and embarrassing.

That memory has been etched in my mind for years – her thinking that I, in any way, would disrespect my grandfather! Fortunately my dad observed what was happening and invited me to join him in the rotunda, where he embraced me and invited me to cry the tears I'd been trying so hard to contain (again, so I wouldn't embarrass my grandmother). As an adolescent with this being the first death of a loved one I'd experienced, that day left some indelible imprints in my mind. Grief became associated with disappointment (my grandmother's in me); and with the expected "paying tribute" to the dead by gazing on Grandpa's lifeless body in his casket.

Years later when my parents passed, the family had long ago agreed on cremation as the way we would honor the dead, and with a memorial service that celebrated their lives, rather than a funeral that seemed to only recognize what was no longer.

Whatever your practice or memories of death, hopefully you can find ways to remember the loved one who has passed by grieving in a creative, rather than a destructive, manner. By that I mean even in the midst of despair you choose to remember and embrace the good times once shared, knowing that that individual's loving energy is still with you to bring comfort and healing in times of sadness. Energy can never be destroyed. What new form may it now take?

A part of you has gone as well, because your relationship with your beloved is no longer. And a relationship takes two. And perhaps the healthiest action you can take at that time of passing or on subsequent occasions of meaning is to let your grief express as you mourn your loss in healthy ways. As Shakespeare reminds us in **Macbeth**, *"Give sorrow words, the grief that does not speak whispers the o'erfraught heart and bids it break."* The unhealthiest thing you can do is to deny or suppress the grief you feel. Feeling held down will emerge with far greater intensity at a later time. Be with your vulnerability, your sorrow, whenever and wherever it may emerge. And it will present at times unexpected, when the love that no longer exists on this physical plane was a powerful presence in your life in earlier times.

If you've never done this before, sometime you might want to write your own obituary. What would you say? What would you want others to remember about you? What songs did you NOT sing when you had the opportunity? And what were you doing at the time of death? This exercise isn't an easy one, but it is a very revealing one. It will reveal how you truly think and feel about yourself. What went unrealized – what talents, convictions, and dreams died with you rather than being expressed? Perhaps the passing of a loved one will invite you to do more, do differently, with your life than you have before. Can you see the world anew at this significant transition point in your life? Allow this particular kind of ending to be a clearing process for you as you very gradually begin to create a new beginning.

We all hold one loss in common, our very first breaking apart. When we were born, our mothers released us from their wombs, where we'd been carried and nurtured for months, into a strange new world that would become our life. At this earliest separation from our beloved, we began our journey of growing in consciousness. Does a new-born infant experience grief? I can't answer that; but I do believe that an infant's birth brings into this world a profound innocence and bliss that best may be expressed in William Wordsworth's words:

> *Our birth is but a sleep and a forgetting:*
> *The Soul that rises with us, our life's Star,*
> *Hath had elsewhere its setting,*
> *And cometh from afar:*
> *Not in entire forgetfulness,*
> *And not in utter nakedness,*
> *But trailing clouds of glory do we come*
> *From God, who is our home;*
> *Heaven lies about us in our infancy!*
> **(Ode: Intimations of Immortality from Recollections of Early Childhood)**

Something is gone, yet another "glory and dream" are being born. Every one of us encounters birth, death, and grief during our lifetime. Growth and healing result when we remain connected to one another and life itself when the going gets tough.

4

BREAKING AN ATTACHMENT

■ ■ ■

Whatever our loss may be – a relationship, a dream, a possession, or a pet - the key to not just surviving but thriving as a result is letting go or surrendering to what occurs. Another way to think about this necessary process is that we should remain detached from people and things this life brings our way. Detachment can be a challenge for us human beings. Change is inevitable. And detachment allows us to experience the freedom that comes from "losing well."

We frequently speak about becoming attached to someone or thing. It's almost as though that person or thing is part of us, like an arm or leg. And although we know the difference, attachment can get us into trouble because we lose our objectivity when we're so close to something that our perspective and judgments become blurred.

Even the idea of attachment suggests cling-i-ness, an unattractive trait that implies neediness. These kinds of feelings are born typically from a sense of insecurity we may have experienced early in life. Fear of loss or abandonment is the implication. Whatever its origin, attachment keeps us from realizing our inherent freedom and independence so that loss of any kind can be devastating. It may also cause us to stay stuck in a state of denial longer than is healthy when someone passes from our life.

Neediness that leads to unhealthy attachments results from a belief that we are not whole without someone or something outside us to complete us. We take past experiences of deprivation or rejection and project them onto a relationship in the hope of healing our neediness. When this illusion dies, we feel betrayed; and our old sense of powerlessness and incompleteness engulfs us, making us feel stripped of all joy and love. Unless and until our false sense of self is recognized, this cycle of dependency and attachment will continue as we seek love outside ourselves. To break such a cycle, first we must recognize the illusion that is causing us to suffer, and then we must let it go – and with it the attachment we've had to another. And this is a choice that will likely need to be made again and again.

I can certainly relate to feelings of not being "good enough" to survive life on my own. Several years into my separation I felt ready to date. I had always lived in relationship, moving from the home of my biological family to the home I made with my husband when I was still in college. Then, some forty-plus years later, I had no home to go to. How could I possibly survive on my own? I'd never had that experience; even in college I lived with a roommate. At sixty years of age I faced a really scary situation. I remember asking women friends who successfully managed living alone how they did it. I was a clueless novice!

Of course there was no magic way to maneuver in this world as a single woman. What it required more than anything else was a strong sense of self and the realization that all I need to thrive on my own exists within me; I didn't need a man or anyone else to complete me. This experience and attendant discovery that *I* was all I needed was very revealing. Yet for the next couple of years my focus and energy remained directed at finding a man with whom to spend the rest of my life. From time to time this effort became an all-consuming task. But the process taught me many things about men in general, and myself in particular.

After a number of fairly serious and love-filled relationships, I met Mr. R. When he and I agreed to separate, I was more okay with myself than I'd ever felt before. The last thing I had any interest in doing was revisiting the dating scene in hopes of finding yet another possible life partner. I had made peace and found love within, finally, to the degree that I knew I was just fine living alone, that I no longer needed someone else to complete me. A lot of self-examination went into this process that lasted about five years. Ultimately I recognized just how much I'd accomplished ON MY OWN, regardless of whether or not I had a man in my life. I was financially and physically strong and healthy, my work was feeding me in important and joyful ways, and I had many men and women friends I could call on for social occasions. I had finally found what I didn't even know I'd been seeking all along – peace of mind that comes with an all-empowering sense of self-worth. And that discovery was entirely an INSIDE JOB!

5

LOVE THAT WILL NEVER DIE

■ ■ ■

Can you imagine how it would feel if you brought forward with you the love (of whatever or whomever) you lost? Although that person, place, or thing is no longer alive, your memories that connect you can be – and be alive in a healthy way. When we remember the love that we once enjoyed, we can allow grieving to expand our consciousness, our awareness, our self-realization. Remember Gibran's words about pain: *"Your pain is the breaking of the shell that encloses your understanding."* This is exactly what the philosopher/poet was saying. As we accept *"the seasons of the heart"* – which ensure us that pain will come as will losses – we can invite love of self and others to grow ever greater, as our lives become more and more inclusive.

Only by staying open and awake to what comes next can we heal the grief over losses we experience. Can we allow our loss to be something that has happened FOR us, rather than TO us? Staying present, reaching out, allowing others in – these are the ways we can overcome and grow stronger.

Ultimately everything – EVERYTHING – is simply energy, just configured differently: some greater mass, some lesser. Energy is indestructible; only form changes. Imagine – as in actively consider – how the love you have lost can be transformed: what new form of energy has it taken?

Writing has been cathartic for me for many years. It may be the same for you. If you've never tried it, take a little time – perhaps on a loved one's birthday or other special occasion; or just when you're feeling low – and write about the good times you remember. Can you use sense memories to again experience a love's presence? Can you allow gratitude to replace regrets, joyful memories to cancel feeling deprived?

Another good reason to write, regardless of whether the loss is due to death or some other reason, is the need for closure. You're not closing off or shutting down your good memories; but you are bringing closure to any unfinished emotional business you may have, or perhaps you're saying good-bye if circumstances precluded that from happening before the break-up. A letter to the lost love can be mailed if that person is still alive but no longer part of your life. And a letter to one who has passed can tie up any lose ends that may need addressing.

To love is to risk feeling hurt, experiencing pain. But remember Shakespeare's wise advice: is it not better to have loved and lost than never to have loved? I often recall these words when someone I know tells me she will never own a pet because she couldn't bear losing it. All I can think of when she expresses this belief is that this person is missing out on a whole lot of love, joy, and companionship – and of the unconditional variety – by short-changing her life in this way. One of my favorite sayings as a dog-lover is that a dog may not be my whole life, but she certainly makes my life whole!

As the Kabbalah teaches, when the heart breaks, it breaks open. As it does, it knows we can transcend the limits of who we believed we were – something has left our life and we feel less than whole because of this loss – as we meet ever greater experiences and expressions of love through our loss. The type of loss we know as death is one of life's greatest mysteries. We will never know how it looks until we personally pass into that energetic experience that exists beyond time and space. But until then, if we allow our essential self (our spiritual self) to grow, we invite the ecstasy of healing to embrace us as we listen quietly to what our heart and soul are teaching us. A heart broken open by grief offers us the opportunity to connect with, to hear, why our soul has brought us to this moment. It's an occasion to master one of this life's biggest lessons!

Part II
Breaking Down

1

WHEN LIFE FALLS APART

■ ■ ■

In Daniel Nahmod's song, ***Unbecoming***, he speaks to how most of us experience this life's journey. Nahmod's lyrics remind me of Wordworth's poem, ***Intimations of Childhood***. Both writers speak about how quickly we forget our divinity, from which we came, and re-brand ourselves in the VERY imperfect humanity the world and those around us convince us we are. But the truth will eventually out, as they say. And when we can finally hide our light no longer, fitting into this world of shadows, we encounter a break-down which leads ultimately to the break-through that allows us to rediscover the Truth about ourselves and our innate magnificence.

An earlier break-up from my husband of forty years was accompanied by my mother's death (a year later); the loss of my spiritual community, a Unity church, which involved both a job loss and the loss of no longer having my church routine and family which had anchored me in many ways; and ultimately the loss of my faith. The combined impact of these life changes took me down to the depths of my being, landing me in a psychiatric hospital due to depression that rendered me unable to cope.

Each of these painful endings, coming one on top of another in the manner they did, took quite some time and energy to overcome. The last was perhaps the most significant and the most challenging: loss of my faith. When that occurred, I was good and truly experiencing a dark night of the soul.

I was formally introduced to spiritual metaphysics at the age of thirty-six, when I began attending a large Unity church. One of the principle tenets of that philosophy, and one to which I continue (despite this interruption) to subscribe, teaches that our most deeply held beliefs shape/create our reality, how we experience this lifetime.

But when I "lost my mind," as I felt I had, I was unable to connect with the God of my being. I had come lose from that which tethered my soul to this body and world. To say I was frightened is to put it mildly. All I knew was that I knew nothing at all. And that is a feeling, an experience, of being ripped apart from all that anchored me to this life.

With the aid of dear friends and professionals, I found the help I needed. But the journey back to myself connected me ultimately to a new beginning, and a new me. Getting to where I was headed involved months of decompressing. The hospitalization experience demonstrated what it feels like to break with (rather than be broken by) any kind of chemical dependency or addiction. I was taken cold-turkey off medically prescribed drugs that had allowed me to cope (though minimally), and escape my days with night-time sleep. Anyone who has suffered with an addiction – I had become addicted to Ambien and couldn't sleep without it – knows how challenging the detoxification process is. In addition I was immediately and completely taken off an anti-depressant which a well-meaning psychiatrist had prescribed in ever increasing dosages. In fact when I was admitted to the hospital, the in-take doctor said he'd never seen such a high dosage of the drug prescribed. No wonder I couldn't cope! But I obviously withstood the rigors of decompression, and not only survived but overcame the pain and losses that had landed me in the hospital.

After months of inpatient living, including living in an all-women dorm with like-disturbed women, I was released to out-patient status. That was terrifying, as I'd come to feel protected and somewhat sure of myself while at the hospital. I was afraid to drive, so I asked my brother to come up to Atlanta from Jacksonville to stay with me for a few weeks. Thankfully he graciously agreed. Once back in familiar surroundings and routines, more quickly than anticipated, I overcame my reluctance to remain holed up and shut down. My brother's visit helped enormously with my quite speedy recovery.

Medication had been a significant culprit in deepening my chronic depression. Now it proved a God-send. The facility where I'd stayed focuses on addiction problems and the psychiatrists there really know their med's. I was put back on Cymbalta, an anti-depressant with which I'd had earlier success. But this time that medication was "jump started" with two additional drugs, Abilify and Seroquel. The cocktail did the trick, but with side effects.

From the time of my marital separation until after my mother's death I had dropped so much weight, from a naturally slim build, that friends said they were frightened for me. I couldn't bear to look in the mirror because all I saw was a skeleton of my former self. Once I started the drug cocktail, I quickly began to regain the weight I'd lost, but unfortunately continued to gain until I was forced to abandon all my clothes for two sizes larger. I'd already taken one costly hit to my wardrobe when I'd dropped one to two sizes the previous year.

I expressed my concern over weight gain, as well as spiking sugar and cholesterol levels with my psychiatrist. He took me off the Abilify and Seroquel as soon as he thought the Cymbalta alone would continue to work. And fortunately, after about six months, it did just that. I continue taking that single anti-depressant, now six years later.

Just as there are different types of depression, there are a variety of causes. My illness added situational depression to chronic depression and dysthymia. Depression may occur as a single, major bout or as recurring episodes over a number of years. Persistent or chronic depressive disorder lasts two years or longer. In my case, this aspect of the disease was first diagnosed when I was in my twenties. Bipolar disorder, or manic-depressive illness, occurs as cycles of depression alternating with extreme highs, or manias.

When I landed in the hospital, situational depression had exacerbated my chronic chemical disorder. Anti-depressant medication is imperative for me. In earlier years I found therapy very helpful. Typically both therapy and medication are prescribed.

Although since Rosalynn Carter as First Lady brought much needed attention to mental health and how it should be treated no differently from any other disease, it continues to be an under-reported and under-treated (or mis-treated) malady. Worldwide, based on *just reported cases*, depression affects over 350 million people, women much more than men. The good news is that this pervasive emotionally and physically disabling disease is treatable. The bad news is that at least as many people, because of ignorance or stigma, do not report symptoms as those who do. In our country alone over 80% of people with symptoms of clinical depression are not receiving any treatment for their disease. This is in part due to lack of insurance coverage for associated mental health costs. A serious related problem occurs when a person stops taking the prescribed med because the individual begins to feel noticeably better. While doctors typically warn their patients to NOT stop taking a drug, many depressed individuals believe they know best. And the result is what happened to me, when first out of my marriage.

And treating depression usually involves a trial and error period, to find out what the right drug is for an individual's system. Unfortunately no tests exist to rule in or rule out various medications. Therefore patience and perseverance are required on the patient's part. At the time I separated from my husband, I was so high, feeling so good from no longer carrying his emotional baggage, that I actually convinced my doctor that I no longer needed to take Cymbalta. He took me off the drug and about six weeks later I began the descent into depression that ultimately led to my hospitalization.

As I gradually "awakened" from my dark night, I knew beyond any doubt that my experience had occurred in order for me to be able to help others in whatever their own recovery processes might look and feel like. And as I began to ascend my ladder to wholeness, day by day the light grew brighter until once again I began to write and teach. Over a five-year period, I gradually invited (energetically) new people, new relationships into my life, and new opportunities into my life. Because I had always lived "in relationship," whether with my biological family or my husband and later our child, I earnestly, and with every ounce of my being, sought a man who would become my new committed partner.

Over several years I met several men with whom I had relationships. I define "relationship" in this sense as an intimate, loving, and (usually) sexual bond that lasted as short as four months and as long as nine. One of those reached the eve of our moving in together, when we both looked at the other in mutual recognition that that was *NOT* the thing to do.

In this instance my break-down was relatively easy and short-lived. For the months during which I'd spent much time at his home, I'd come to clearly envision where and how my furniture and accessories would fit when it became OUR home. During the month before my movers were scheduled, we already had moved clothes, dishes, plants, and other items we could carry in our cars. When we realized our plans were not going to materialize, we had to once again load up our cars and make many trips in the reverse direction.

The deep sadness I experienced over this loss was more about the MOVE not happening than it was about losing the man. Because I knew I hadn't lost him, but I had most definitely lost my dream of living with him for the rest of our lives. He and I continued as friends with benefits, never once doubting the wisdom of our decision.

It's so much easier when two people agree, reach the same conclusion at the same time, that a break-up is incumbent. It's more difficult when one alone utters the ultimatum and the other feels as though a kick-punch to the gut has been delivered. Truth is, whether you're the partner giving or receiving that kick, both people hurt (assuming there was something substantive to the relationship in the first place). I've been in both places, and I'm not sure which was more difficult.

While break-ups continued in my life as a single adult, the time and intensity I spent in the break-down period lessened with each succeeding episode. As had been the case with my depression, I put into practice all that I had learned, enabling myself to have an easier time with whatever challenge faced me. The most difficult break-up AND break-down as a single woman occurred, however, with the relationship I had before I met Mr. R.

I was in the process of writing **Outrageous Loving!** at the time. And about midway through that book, I came to a standstill. That happened when my last two relationships overlapped. When the second man entered my life, I was deeply in love and enjoying an affair (neither of us married) with a man whose life's philosophy and spiritual beliefs were too different from my own for us to make a lasting commitment. We both recognized this truth, and had agreed to just enjoy all the good things we could share for as long as that was possible. For us both, it became impossible way too soon.

I have described what happened in depth in my earlier writing, so I will simply summarize here. Mr. R was someone I had known in an earlier lifetime. He and I both recognized that fact and believed we were being given an opportunity to resolve any karmic issues that remained between us. In the process of writing **Outrageous Loving!**, I was living what I was writing about – loving and enjoying an intimate relationship with two men at the same time. Ultimately I had to choose one over the other. I chose Mr. R, and from an earlier chapter, you know what happened!

Yet as much as I missed the relationship I gave up, I knew I had made the right decision. And even though my former lover has moved on into another affair, we stay in touch and remain good friends.

Perhaps one reason I can deal with loss more easily, although not any less painfully, than some is my belief that we live more than one lifetime. Whether those lives, or other expressions of our consciousness, are sequential or co-exist in "parallel universes" I do not know. But I believe that my consciousness, which ultimately merges with what I call God consciousness (the source of all that is) and which unites us all as one, is **much** greater than my expression and experience as Susan in this 21st century on planet Earth. Therefore since God/Love/ Creative Energy is the ultimate Life Force, when I "lose" a loved one, of whatever nature, I know that our energetic connection continues. It is not something that manifests and can be seen, felt or in any other way experienced with my physical senses. But our energy fields will always be joined and as they are, although my loss is no longer experienced at this human level of existence, I know its life continues. And hopefully continues at a higher level or degree of awareness.

Consciousness studies, such as those done at IONS – The Institute of Noetic Sciences – as well as the scientific work being done by quantum physicists and other interested parties, are exploring at depth our ultimate energetic connectivity. The great news is that FINALLY science and spirituality are no longer at odds. I distinguish "spirituality" from "religion" in the following way. Spirituality is a belief system, similar to a philosophy, that guides people in ways that lead them to a productive, positive, happy lifestyle. Religion consists of dogma, ritual, and often a number of do's and don'ts and typically brings like-minded folks together in regular services. Many religions exist and often, unfortunately, emphasize the differences rather than the similarities they share with other faiths.

2

BECOMING INTIMATE WITH FEAR

■ ■ ■

When things fall apart, when you break down after a separation or loss, you can experience a kind of healing through this time of testing. And you can come out on the other side having not just survived, but having overcome. Healing results from a combination of grief and relief, misery as well as joy. At times such as these we can either awaken or fall more deeply into sleep. When we strike out at ourselves, at our God, at someone whom we blame, the pain and angst only worsen. We see that happening all around us in the world, every day. Anger explodes and fuels more pain and an angrier than ever response. This becomes a cycle hard to end; but, yes, there is a better way, for us as individuals and for our world.

The deeply disturbing events that may plunge us down the rabbit hole happen for a reason. The simplest reason is they are a call to awaken from the sleep-walking that has become habitual. As Ecclesiastes reminds us, there's a season for every matter under heaven. We cycle through seasons of activity and growth, offset by times of rest and renewal. With the constancy of change, we might never awaken and grow. It's paradoxical but true that we can simultaneously experience grief and joy, opposite sides of the same coin.

But during this down time we often feel only the pain and uncertainty – the fear – of the transition, and we're left to do our best to cope. Challenging as such times can be, try always to remember that they are offering us an opportunity for transformation into a new and more powerful way of being in this world. An ending is also a new beginning.

So long as we fear and resist change, we will stay stuck. Because our ego is a champion of the status quo, that resistance can sometimes operate at an unconscious level, as we sabotage our own efforts to progress in healthy ways. We fear change, and yet change is inevitable. As Robert Brumet says in ***Finding Yourself in Transition*** (Unity House, 2001, p.20), *"change often takes us into new territory where old maps are no longer sufficient."* That was certainly the case when I'd lost both my husband and my mother. That time of great loss demanded that I create a new road map that would show me a new way to travel on my spiritual journey.

Our most common fears, those all of us share, are fear of change and fear of death (some even include fear of public speaking). It's of great benefit to explore and challenge what each of these fears means for us, what they imply, the mysteries behind them, and the ways in which we can turn such fears into friends. Intimate ones at that! But in order to accomplish that, we must accept that our life is a process, a natural one at that. We seldom move in a linear progression, however. Rather, there are ups and down, we move forward and then backward. And that's just fine; it's the "natural way" to DO life. We like to be able to predict outcomes, what comes next, rather than simply trusting the innate divine wisdom of our process. The end goal of that process is to LIVE CONSCIOUSLY, while most of us continue to function in a largely unconscious manner, running through our days on auto-pilot. Always remember that because our life is a process, we will change over time, not over night!

I've always loved the Chinese meaning for the word CRISIS: a combination of danger and opportunity. When we become able to see the meaning in and of our discomfort as we find ourselves in crisis, we will invite the break-through that such challenge offers us. Key to making our fear our friend is recognizing that it is our resistance to fear that makes it our enemy. Resisting, of course, means holding on; in the instances we're examining, that means holding on to something or someone we have lost. And while memories can be very worthwhile and serve us well, trying to perpetuate something that no longer is creates resistance to moving forward into a new beginning. When we are able to accept an ending as a new beginning, as part of our life's process, we become able to live and love and thrive at a greater level than ever before.

When we lose something familiar, it feels as though we've lost some part of ourself, our identity is no longer what it has been. But as we release this ego need to hold on, to resist change, we can become more of who we truly are – an individual not defined, not confined, by what life outside says we are. It may be difficult, but can you imagine grief as the process through which we are healed? Grieving a loss is a major step in coming "home" to our higher Self.

Each of us tends to live within a certain set of expectations (largely based on past experiences), values, and identities (someone's daughter, someone's wife, someone's mother, someone's employee, someone's boss, someone's sister, etc.). When one of those pieces of us as defined by roles in this world, and when our ego is shaken or shattered by an ending, we may feel broken, certainly bereft, and at times, unable to go on with our own life. In ***In Midlife***, Murray Stein calls this space we find ourselves in "psychological liminality": *"(it) occurs when the ego is separated from a fixed sense of who it is and has been, of where it comes from and its history, of where it is going and its future; when the ego is (separated) from the inner images that have formerly sustained it and given it a sense of purpose."*(Spring Publishing, 1988, p.22). Our life's direction has been disrupted. Fear is the result.

As was my case shortly before hospitalization, more than anything else, I wanted, I tried, to turn to God. But all I could sense was separation; and great distress was the result. Just as earlier I had felt God shaking the foundation of my life so I would end my marriage and move onward to a greater way of being, ironically as I followed where that move would lead, my very faith in God was shaken. In fact, it was no more. And without the beliefs that had always sustained and enriched my life, how could I continue living? What I would discover, after I came through this dark night of my soul, was that God, yet again, was seeking to express more fully through me.

During the tumultuous time of breaking down, we likely feel the way T.S. Eliot describes this stage of life in *Four Quartets*:

To arrive where you are, to get from where you are not,
You must go by a way wherein there is no ecstasy.
In order to arrive at what you do not know
You must go by a way which is the way of ignorance.
In order to possess what you do not possess
You must go by the way of dispossession.
In order to arrive at what you are not
You must go through the way in which you are not.
And what you do not know is the only thing you know
And what you own is what you do not own
And where you are is where you are not.

To sum up, nothing seems quite real at this stage of a break-down. In our state of feeling helpless and abandoned, thoughts of death may creep in. As we seek to avoid such fears, addiction and dysfunctional behavior may enter the picture. We seek to defend, to protect, ourselves and become vulnerable as we do. We seek to resist feeling fearful by numbing ourselves through drink, drugs, non-stop television, sexual permissiveness, eating, sleeping, or some other means of dying to the day. This time of emptiness is fearful; we dare not trust it. So we resist, attempting to fill it with a distraction such as those just mentioned. Life feels both empty and chaotic; and we forget that chaos is always a harbinger to life and a new beginning. The more we resist the feelings of this break-down, the longer they will persist.

In another verse from *The Prophet* Gibran tells us, *"And could you keep your heart in wonder at the daily miracles of your life, your pain would not seem less wondrous than your joy."* How true and yet how challenging! Emotions are so volatile and our perspective so blurred at this time, that making major decisions should be avoided. Above all, don't attempt to rush this part of the process, this stage of life. Don't try to go back to old ways of doing life, as they probably won't work. Do your best to JUST BE, in this moment, present to this passage. Call on supportive friends who understand the value of this transition, because they have been where you are now and are witnesses to what lies ahead. Find ways to express your deepest feelings, however dark they may be. Talk with your soul to the extent you can pray and meditate. Allow yourself to just be still. And listen to that still small voice inside that is your higher wisdom and greatest guide.

Release whatever, however, the old way was and looked. Days and feelings and experiences will vacillate between what was and the new consciousness and awareness that is being born. Let your loss teach you what this time of life has come to do. Know that you will regain connection to your Source that you feel as though you have lost, and trust that you are being guided every step of the way.

Life is in Divine Order, whatever is occurring. And the time it takes will be as long as it takes! Do you remember the story in *Exodus* about Moses leading the Israelites from Egypt and their enslavement under Pharaoh to the Promised Land? The process, their journey, took forty years. Metaphysically, the number forty means "as long as it takes." I have always been fascinated and somewhat amazed that my marriage ended in our fortieth year together.

For me becoming intimate with my fears took the experience of a total mental and emotional break-down. But that probably could have been avoided if, rather than fighting the depression, I had not resisted with tooth and nail as I did. Yes, there were extenuating circumstances, such as seeing a therapist not equipped to knowledgeably deal with medications. But with me, what happened was what needed to happen.

Sometimes the word "fear" is seen as an acronym for "false events/experiences appearing real." When you're gripped by any kind of fear, large or small, remembering this saying may help you shake yourself lose. After all, there are ultimately only two emotions, fear and love. Since they cannot co-exist, choose the real one, love, and see how quickly you can banish your fear! And remember that the only way to overcome is to ride through it – whatever IT may be. That's the path to true awakening. Practice peace, not war. And as you do this on an individual basis, you will be helping not only yourself, but our world as well.

3

GIVING UP THE NEED TO CONTROL OUR FEARS

■ ■ ■

If you're anything like me, having grown up in a dysfunctional house-hold, control became a necessary way of trying to maintain or regain balance in situations that had become unbalanced. I'm also a pusher, a Type A personality/ego that wants what I want, and wants it right now. I expect you've heard the version of the Serenity Prayer that says, "God, give me peace, and give it to me right now!" That was my prayer for many years. Today I continue to work on releasing these old habitual routines of controlling and pushing. Frankly, they're quite exhausting, and when others are involved, as they typically are, very annoying as well.

Society does a very effective job of "domesticating" us, by which I mean we unconsciously adopt many beliefs and ways of operating in this world by what others – peers, superiors, news media, etc. – tell us are the correct ways to behave. What we deem right or wrong, good or bad, is a result of external influences and the results experiences have dealt us. In fact everything in life is ultimately neutral until we, indi-vidually and collectively, put a value on it.

So let's look more deeply at our fears about loss, whether it's the ultimate loss to death or some other less "final" break-up. Buddhism tells us that we will no longer experience fear when we can accept the truth that impermanence, change, and even hopelessness are keys to being at peace in the world. While it's fairly easy and straightforward to acknowledge that impermanence and change certainly happen, how can hopelessness possibly bring us peace?

Before reading further, think about what "hoping" something does or does not happen means. Until we give up hope – which sounds like both a daunting and a dismal idea – we can't possibly relax with where or who we are. Hoping means there's something better to be, someone better to be with, somewhere better to live, a better job, and on and on. Such hoping creates a restlessness and sense of dissatisfaction with the status quo. Maybe that's why ego so abhors change! (That's a joke I hope you get).

In her book **When Things Fall Apart**, American Buddhist nun Pema Chodron makes this distinction between theism (belief in a God) and nontheism: *"Theism is a deep-seated conviction that there's some hand to hold: if we just do the right things, someone will appreciate us and take care of us. It means thinking there's always going to be a babysitter available when we need one. We are all inclined to abdicate our responsibilities and delegate our authority to something outside ourselves. Nontheism is relaxing with the ambiguity and uncertainly of the present moment without reaching for any-thing to protect ourselves."*(Shambhala, 2000, p.39)

While the concept of God as babysitter was a new one for me, it certainly rings true. It's the idea that we need, and therefore believe in, something or someone **outside ourselves** to measure up to; and some-one to take care of us in challenging times; something to hold onto when we're struggling to hold on. Nontheism recognizes that there is no babysitter we can count on, because they come and go. And all life is just that way: things and people come and go. Impermanence is a rule of life, and it's a truth that's often inconvenient and unpleasant to real-ize. Life is life. There's love and loss; joy and pain. As Chodron points out, we're all addicted to hope. Hope that doubt, mystery, and all things we consider "bad" will disappear.

I never thought of HOPE and FEAR as two sides of the same coin. But when introduced to that idea, I understood it clearly. Both feelings suggest that we lack something; and due to that sense of impoverishment, we can't relax. If you never considered that HOPE could be a negative, read on. When holding on to hope, we can't be present to this moment, to NOW. Something or someone is missing and are necessary in order for us to feel complete and able to be at peace. But that very notion that something is missing, a fear, convinces us that something better can exist, can happen. And we hold on to the hope it will. Hope robs us of all we DO have, this very moment. The compassionate thing to do, the thing that will make us feel good at this very moment so that we CAN relax and feel at peace, is to acknowledge that RIGHT NOW we feel like crap. And we shouldn't mind taking a good hard look at why we feel that way. We should be courageous and brave and as Chodron so eloquently puts it, "…smell that piece of sh_t….feel it; (examine) its texture, color, and shape." We can know its nature and not be embarrassed or feel shame. We can drop the hope that a "better me" will emerge some day.

The message is loud and clear: when we take a straight and unadulterated look at what's going on in our life, at all our hopes and fears, some kind of confidence in our basic sanity comes forth. We can accept that what is, is. When we renounce any hope that things could be better if our experience were different, we're on our way to expunging fear from any sense we have of self or life.

Earlier I mentioned how we may use (often abuse) alcohol, sex and so on – babysitters – to escape the present moment, which includes fear. What we're doing is using these distractions to let go of the tenacious hope we have that we can be saved from being who we are. Our fear, and our hope, if we're fortunate, can be teachers that inspire us to investigate what's going on when we reach for something outside ourselves because we're too frightened to face what's coming.

Our ultimate fear is fear of death. And fear of death is always in the background of whatever fear we're experiencing. Why deny fear of death? It's going to happen. We're all impermanent in our human garb, as is everything in our human world. Western society more than most teaches us to fear death; as children we're often hidden from it because it's deemed the ultimate worst thing that can ever happen. Yet when we accept its inevitability, we can be at peace. After all, death and change are certainties, and our only certainties.

Another, perhaps more palatable, way to explain this Buddhist idea about HOPE is by using the word ACCEPTANCE. When we're willing to accept what is, we can be at peace and in this moment. That's the positive spin, and the one I prefer and expect the same is true for you. So what happens when we truly relax into the knowing of death's inevitability? For me, that acceptance allows me to also accept other kinds of death: getting old, getting sick, losing someone or something I love. Face it: things end. And once we become so comfortable with ourselves that we can live a joy-filled life, we no longer ignore or deny the reality of impermanence, of death – of all kinds.

4

WHERE THERE'S PAIN, THERE'S GAIN

■ ■ ■

But we never seem to realize that truth when we're in the midst of our pain. Before we entered this lifetime, our soul knew the lessons we needed to master. And the experiences that would help them unfold in our lives to ensure our maximum learning potential. And everything in our lives has perfectly positioned us for the service we are here to perform and our potential for growth.

The Persian poet Rumi tells us not to grieve, that *"anything you lose comes round in another form."* Would that we would remember this Truth during our darkest days. The fears that gripped me following the loss of my marriage and my mother weren't so much about danger as they were my sense that I'd become disconnected from the God of my being. Everything in my life in those days seemed out of kilter. I couldn't even drive myself, I was so discombobulated. It was as if the loss of these two extremely important and much loved individuals held me hostage, frozen and unable to manage my own life. So deeply had my mind become rooted in a sense of separation and illusion, I was living as a ghost of my real self, incomplete and completely lost. Or so it seemed. Had some entity taken hold of me, sucking out all my energy and inner resources?

I was experiencing a storm, a tsunami of grief, and at the same time resisting it. A sure recipe for disaster. The eye of a hurricane is a place of perfect calm. Even while the storm rages all around it, creating devastation, that eye is still and peaceful. Had I been non-resistant to the depression I was experiencing at that time, I am convinced the entire ordeal would have played out differently from the way it did. The way we choose to relate to our experiences is the way they become. Our emotional response to our circumstances arises from what we make the situation mean. My frame of reference to the world had become grossly distorted. A kind of blindness was getting in the way of my seeing a healthy outcome and the possibility that I would in fact GAIN from this time of pain.

Things that influence how we react, or respond, to circumstances include memories and how we feel about ourselves. When you feel lost and alone, unable to function in healthy ways, ask yourself what your sense of worth is. How do you feel about yourself? What do you deserve at this time of loss? Self-examination is key to becoming present to life and re-gaining the center, the balance, you seem to have lost. What supports your insecurity, your fear, your defensiveness and co-dependency needs? What beliefs have frozen you in this moment of indecision, dysfunction, and paralysis?

Any time we use our condition or situation as evidence of our well-being and worth, we become more or less than our Truth because of what is happening around us. We have given away our power, our ability to choose because of a sense of unworthiness and ineptitude. Transforming times of challenge to experiences that can empower us takes courage and inner strength. They are situations that demand we call on our inner resources for comfort and guidance. Any time we face adversity, the Universe is trying to get our attention, trying to help us recognize that the imbalance, incongruity, and self-deception we experience is rooted deeply in our subconscious. And it's up to us to redefine ourselves and our circumstances in ways that will serve us in the highest ways possible. Only WE hold our own well-being hostage!

Our doubts and insecurities – how can we go on living with the loss we've suffered – reveal themselves not as weaknesses so much as areas of potential, expansion, and awakening. When we're willing to venture to the edge of what feels like our safety, to gaze into the abyss, awakening to what Life is offering us becomes a real possibility. We must confront our fears, not run away or hide from them. Only in the presence of challenge can we awaken to the greater possibilities the opportunity is offering. For most of us, we remain separated from parts of ourselves that have yet to be integrated into our sense of wholeness and well-being. Our fears, judgments, false beliefs, and limiting ideas must be examined – honestly examined – and be integrated with our self-concept in order for us to realize just how whole and perfect we are, each in a divine, perfect, and unique way.

When we struggle with conditions that challenge or threaten us – including losses – we not only reinforce their presence in our lies, we also block our spiritual growth and development. Resistance of any kind produces discomfort, stress, and grief. A little science reinforces this idea. Resistance is the property of conductivity of an electrical conductor. Ohm's Law of Resistance tells us that the amount of current flowing through an electrical conductor is inversely proportional to the amount of resistance in the wire. So when resistance is high, current flow is low; conversely, when resistance is close to zero, current flow has the potential to reach infinity.

Resistance clogs our energy channels, greatly diminishing our ability to both receive and then act on those ideas and desires that feed us in positive ways. Feelings of unworthiness and inadequacy keep us from experiencing love and fulfillment. Resistance in consciousness can come from thoughts, feelings, or beliefs. When we either tend to push away bad feelings or cling to good ones, old coping strategies interfere with our ability to heal and grow. Any time we wish something were different from what it is, we're giving more power to the situation.

Resistance, challenge, and even conflict are necessary elements in our lives because such conditions stretch us and help us discover new dimensions within ourselves and in others. What we need to do is avoid personalizing these aspects of our humanity. Because of old messages – many of which are parts of the race consciousness – we assume when confronted by what we believe are "negative" situations, that something is wrong, something is to be avoided. Resistance can make us stronger or it can weaken us. Our choice!

Think about what makes a relationship either healthy or unhealthy. Once you do that, I believe you will be better able to deal with any kind of loss that enters your life. When first born we move out of a sense of connection (in our mother's womb) to that of separation, as we learn through trial and error to function independently. At the same time we quickly move into codependent relationships with many of the people in our lives. All of us are born into an imperfect care-giving environment. Because as infants and very young children we don't have the perspective and experience base from which to understand and ground us in reality, we must look outside ourselves for evidence and interpretations regarding what is happening all around us.

As we age and gain sufficient experience to form our own opinions and perceptions about life, if we still depend on others in order to feel okay about ourselves, we are continuing relationships of codependency. As a codependent, we rely heavily on what others think, do and say to the way WE relate to the world. As I glanced at this morning's local paper I couldn't miss the lead front page story, accompanied by a photograph. A large home in a neighboring community had burned from the inside out. The headline read, *"They're dead; my whole life is over."* Indeed, tragedy had struck a young family of four when the father was the only survivor of an unexplained fire that had taken the lives of his wife and two daughters. The fire's cause was as yet undetermined.

It's a gross understatement to say this man, husband, and father had experienced a tremendous loss. What struck me, however, were the words he used to express his tragedy. And while it may not have been hyperbole in this moment of almost inexpressible grief, the statement caused me to examine once again our personal relationships. When we lose family members to death, regardless of the cause, the pain can be overwhelming. And the need to grieve and all the related steps of moving through such loss are extremely important.

We become separated from our core essence, our essential Self, early on because of the events and circumstances that influence us. We learn how to control others, avoid conflict, resist change, and be right (at the expense of happiness). We learn that loving someone sometimes hurts. And with all this learning the ways of the world, how it is to be human, we forget our own worth and find a sense of well-being outside ourselves. As all these ways of being in the world happen, we become attached to and highly vested in outcomes. We learn to manage our fears by manipulating and controlling others and situations, which in turn creates conflicts that lead to ever greater dependence on others for what we seem to be missing in ourselves. THINGS become the measure of our happiness and worth. We lose whatever sense of authenticity we once had.

Soon we are living on auto-pilot, a mode dependent on resistance, attachment, defensiveness, the need to be right, and the need to control others. Break-downs occur because we become unable to experience communion, or connectedness, with ourselves and others, and we lose any sense of connection we once had with God. Instead of assuming responsibility for our lives, we abdicate any sense of accountability to others. In effect we give away our God-given power to manage our lives in ways that bring us peace and contentment.

In this boxed-in way we learn to live, based on what we perceive outside and all around us, our perspective becomes severely limited. It is not only limited, and limiting, it is self-serving and piecemeal.

5

LONELINESS: ANOTHER KIND OF DEATH

■ ■ ■

As I remember my times of deep depression, I realize how alone I felt. No longer did I have my husband and marriage, the security I'd known for so many years. I'd lost my church home and community that brought me so much joy and sense of fulfillment. I no longer had either parent, and my siblings lived miles away. My son was grown and on his own, an adult with his own (separate from me) life. I'd lost the comforts of my home, which I'd enjoyed and in which I felt secure and contented for so long. I'd even lost many of the friendships my spouse and I had cultivated over the years. I did indeed feel very lonely. Most frightening was my sense that I'd lost my faith, and with it, everything that meant anything in my life. And until I discovered a new, a different, kind of relationship with myself, I would continue to feel alone, abandoned, and deeply depressed.

I was unable to even access old and familiar ways to escape discomfort: sleep (I became addicted to Ambien as the only way my mind would turn off); alcohol (drink no longer relieved my pain); people (I was so distraught I was unable to reach out to another for help). So in the depths of my dark night, I couldn't even move; and yet I didn't want to be still and just feel what I needed to feel. Had I been able to be at peace with my pain and loneliness, no doubt I would have overcome my depression in a less debilitating way. Instead I found myself in the most uncomfortable place of all, in hospital detox.

How might have this process of "detox" looked, and felt, had I not been distressed by my feelings of loneliness and uncertainty – accepting the (painful) Truth that there's no certainty about anything; and I don't ultimately know anything! That basic truth hurt, and I wanted to escape it. But I was cheating myself by seeking an alternative, running away from my loneliness and sense of emptiness.

Society and all the influences that teach us what is *good* and *bad, right* and *wrong*, tend to convince us that anything that makes us uncomfortable, any difficulty that arises in our lives, we should try to get rid of. We habitually struggle against whatever is happening to us or in us. We're seldom, if ever, encouraged to move into, toward, difficulties rather than away from them. How would life be radically different if we viewed these times, such as times of loneliness, as a means of awakening to a greater sense of who we are, of what life is meant to be? Our greatest challenge is to overcome the fear of moving TOWARD the things we find most difficult, the things we seek so desperately to avoid. A wise student/teacher once said, "Lower your standards and relax as it is." If only we would learn to do just that!

When something occurs in life that hurts, we seldom see it as a good thing, as a source of wisdom, a great teaching from which we can learn important lessons. Rather, we tend to see painful situations as things we want to escape. Our greatest challenge is to learn from this moment, from whatever is occurring right now, to cease labeling life's events as *good* or *bad, right* or *wrong*. How we relate to this present moment, whatever we may be experiencing, creates our future. Our future is what we do right now!

Part III
Breaking Through

1

DON'T JUST SURVIVE, THRIVE!

■ ■ ■

As we begin to be "okay" after our foundation has been shaken, perhaps even collapsed, we've taken the first step to no longer resisting what Life has brought up to help us heal. What we once viewed as tragedy we can now see as an opportunity for growth. Rather than feeling fearful, we now welcome such situations in anticipation. As our perceptions and understanding about "good" and "bad," "right" and "wrong," shift, our world becomes much more manageable, and we personally are able to more fully relax into what *IS*. Worry about what *MAY BE* no longer keeps us awake at night. And most important, we are now learning to be not just okay, but great, fabulous, with who we are and the life we are attracting to us.

As we break through into this "new day" that promises so much, we've done more than survive whatever loss we may have experienced. Rather, we have overcome; and in our overcoming, we are thriving. We've come home to our true Self, our Higher Self, and are learning to trust that whatever happens, a divine plan is at work in our lives and in the life of our world and planet. Knowing that all is well, we have ceased needing to control life's circumstances and other people; we no longer "push" to make Life happen on our schedule, which is often unhealthy, as we allow it to flow and open according to its nature; and we no longer resist, but rather surrender to what is. At the same time, we are living a life that invites us to share all we know and be all we are in ways that inspire confidence and faith that the Universe knows exactly what It is doing!

We've come to accept the Truth that everything in our outer world is impermanent, and our definitions of "security" and "stability" have radically changed from what they were originally. Those things that once seemed paradoxical and ambiguous – such as *an ending is a beginning* – now make sense. Words including *surrender* and *non-attachment* are now more clearly understood with regard to our experiences, circumstances, and relationships.

So let's examine in detail how we have matured in ways that make us what we can call a master, a sage. Richard Bach, in his beloved book ***Illusions***, writes that *"What the caterpillar calls the end of the world, the master calls a butterfly."* Now as you re-examine the losses you have gone through, you can hopefully have the perspective that Lao Tsu explained when he wrote, *"Because the sage always confronts difficulties, he never experiences them."*

2

INTERNAL CHANGES

■ ■ ■

I believe that before we can see changes in the outer, we must experience them on the inner. And such internal experiences can feel like God is shaking the very foundation of our being; or they can be as subtle as a butterfly flitting its wings as it perches on our shoulder. The important point is that whether it's gentle or tsunami-like, we GET IT – that inner shift, an inner awakening, that signals a new beginning is on its way.

Chaos always precedes creation. In fact, it is an inherent part of the creative process. As such we can expect disturbances of sometimes turbulent proportions when we are on the verge of our most significant discoveries or revelations. Keep in mind that the more severe the challenge you're facing, the more enormous the potential break-through. Certain stressors and the times they occur can be more trying than others. When we experience trauma as infants or young children, our vulnerability may cause those ordeals to be buried at the unconscious level of our mind. When that happens, an event later in life may trigger the anger, grief, or pain (emotional and sometimes physical) that exhibits at that time. Often such occurrences are unexplainable, so deeply hidden are the original issues. Part of our journey as souls that are evolving is this process of bringing into conscious awareness what has been hidden at the unconscious level.

As a VERY important early step as you recover and move toward your new beginning, ASK YOURSELF THIS ALL-IMPORTANT QUESTION: *Do you love yourself enough to let go of those things that no longer serve you?* "Things" include but are not necessarily limited to the following: people, values, beliefs, memories, expectations, control, judgments, desires, and needs. STOP; take a long, deep breath. Just be with this question. The time you give yourself to consider it will be your first clue – do you, or do you not, love yourself enough….?

Until you literally put 100% of your focus on the question and all that it brings forth for you – one consideration at a time – you won't know whether or not you're awake enough to embrace the good that awaits you. When I do this exercise, it's never easy; it often means I really have to dig down deep into the recesses of my mind to uncover old messages and memories that cause me discomfort. The way I proceed is as follows. Something today, right now, is making me uncomfortable. What exactly is it? I need to get as clear as possible about that experience. Who said or did something upsetting? And then I start to dig: WHY does this situation make me so uncomfortable?

For example, last night my partner expressed his dismay that I'd turned down the thermostat to a comfortable sleeping temperature for *ME*. Unfortunately (or not?), he and I have opposing needs when it comes to our home's temperature, both day and night. This has been an on-going challenge. Because his comment made me uncomfortable, I began to examine why I felt upset. And for the next hour or so I asked myself a number of questions, such as these. This is MY home and this man is living here as a guest; so why do I feel like his needs/preferences are more important than my own? What does his being a MAN have to do with my concern, if anything? How do I REALLY feel about our relationship? What am I afraid will happen if I don't meet his need (for a warmer home)? And last, something that should have been first, WHAT ABOUT SUSAN?

As I took this internal inventory and reviewed my history, I was reminded *once again* (remember, growth is a process!) to LOVE MYSELF ENOUGH…. And of course I'm talking about a self-Love, and Self-love, love that has nothing whatever to do with narcissism or hubris. It's more about respect, respect for WHO and WHAT I am according to the beliefs I hold dear about myself and my relationship with the Universe. Clearly there remain deep-seated, unconscious beliefs that undermine what my day-to-day awareness preaches, teaches, and lives to the best of my ability.

So again, I ask you – do you love yourself enough to let go of those things that no longer serve you, that limit your growth, that stand in the way of your success and true happiness? It's a question you may want to ask yourself any and every time something or someone causes you discomfort. The time you spend digging (!) for the answers will be the best-spent time you'll ever take. That's my promise to you! If you really wish to confront your fears and challenge your beliefs to expand your understanding and grow, get ready for an incredible journey. Never fear to fly higher because when you're ready, you'll never fall. Push the edges that are the boundaries you've created to supposedly keep you safe and secure, while keeping your fears at bay. It's those very edges that have kept you trapped and limited, kept you from bringing forth and sharing your God-given gifts.

As previously unconscious parts of your internal map come into conscious awareness, you may experience discomfort, confusion, and other unpleasant symptoms. This awareness is the beginning of the end of your ability to continue acting from thoughts or behavior that no longer serve you. Discomfort occurs because holding on to old habits has somehow brought you a sense of security, and ego does not like to rock the boat! It's time to make a change, and the bigger the implications of said change, the greater ego struggles to maintain the status quo.

Physical symptoms, emotions, thoughts, and feelings become so strong that you can no longer suppress or deny that something significant is going on at an internal level. The most important response is to not deny those uncomfortable feelings, but rather to acknowledge them as part of the change process. When I was studying Emily Cady, a late eighteenth/early nineteenth century holistic practitioner and Unity teacher, I became familiar with the experience she called *chemicalization*.

Although somewhat old-fashioned, that term is very descriptive of what's going on inside as we're making significant changes in our beliefs and related habits. In Unity's glossary, chemicalization is defined as a *"condition of the mind that is brought about by the conflict that takes place when a high spiritual realization contacts an old error state of consciousness."* In other words, when old thoughts and habits no longer serve us, we experience discomfort, or upheaval, at mental and physical levels (internal responses) until we allow what's happening to be okay and become non-resistant to it. That means we must not allow our conscious mind to numb-out through distractions such as food, television, drugs and alcohol, sex, or similar diversions during this process of change.

During this time your awareness expands and you begin to recognize how old patterns have created suffering for you. Remember: core beliefs do manifest in our lives, out-picturing as our experiences. To determine what your core beliefs really are, all you need to do is observe what is happening in your life. For example, if you're creating unhappy relationships, the core belief might be some version of "No one will ever love me" or "I am unlovable." Another clue to gain clarity about core beliefs is to listen to your self-talk when you're feeling desperate or unhappy. If you hear something like "No matter what I do, it's never good enough," what does that tell you about yourself? Low self-esteem, perhaps?

When we turn the spotlight on ourselves in these ways, we take responsibility for what we're creating in our lives and in our world. There are no external forces to blame. We create our experiences with our conscious AND unconscious thoughts, especially the habitual or repetitive ones. This process is all about bringing into conscious awareness what has been held unconscious. It's neither comfortable nor easy; but it's very necessary for growth to occur. You are recognizing that you've reached a point of chaos, or crisis, and are now ready to reorganize your mind at a higher level. Once you bring full awareness to a feeling or behavior that doesn't support your life currently (that is, it creates suffering for you), that feeling will be replaced by something that does work for you.

I will return now to an idea I addressed earlier because it's such an important activity to master for anyone on the path of spiritual growth. In a nutshell the secret – and something only you can do – is STOP TRYING TO CONTROL SO RESISTANCE WILL GO AWAY. Believe it or not, resistance is the cause of all our discomfort. So if we can eliminate resistance, we eliminate discomfort. It's that simple - just not quite as easy as it sounds.

Step one: recognize resistance when it occurs. This step requires that you move into the role of witness, or observer. It may sound silly, but the next time, any time, you feel uncomfortable, just notice what's going on. When you JUST NOTICE, you don't try to make the discomfort disappear, for that's just adding more resistance to the problem. You'll be trying to control the situation, not simply observing it. The more you practice being the witness/observer, the easier it will be to assume that role. The secret is to LET WHAT IS BE OKAY; don't fight it or try to make it disappear.

When consciously on a path of growth you will experience more discomfort than if you're hiding from growth. When you choose to observe rather than resist what's happening, you may feel intensity, but it will be neutral intensity rather than negative intensity. What does that mean? Experiences can be positive, negative, or neutral, depending on whether we welcome them, resist them, or are ambivalent about them. How we feel depends on the meaning we place on the experience. Therefore, when we don't resist an intense experience, we won't have a negative experience of it. Just let what happens be okay! Resistance, as we've seen earlier, is never a good thing. Simply being okay means acknowledging something, being present with it, and making your peace with the fact that it is the experience you're having. Discomfort doesn't have to be a negative experience. Growth implies times of overwhelm as we advance our personal growth.

3

LIFE AS THE OBSERVER

■ ■ ■

Living life as an observer, or witness, of ourselves is the way to move through any loss or change painlessly. That doesn't mean we'll never feel sad or experience any other emotions natural to being a human; but it does guarantee that we won't suffer. We won't suffer because living the life of a witness means we give up attachment. Being attached to certain outcomes causes pain and suffering. And we learn how being attached makes us feel at an early age.

Our culture is one of mass meaning: early on we become used to having others interpret our lives for us. Even as children we forget our inherent power to choose for ourselves, which would enable us to take control of our lives rather than letting external influences do that for us. But even as we age and have experiences that SHOULD help us think for ourselves, too often we don't.

Each of us is powerful beyond what we can imagine. We can gain an understanding of that power, and reclaim it, by first recognizing that we give EVERYTHING any and all the meaning it has: there is no intrinsic meaning to anything. Every being and every event is neutral until we ascribe meaning and value to it – good or bad, right or wrong, beautiful or ugly, and so on. And most of these meanings we subscribe to according to conventions of our culture, our families, and other influences that have been part of our lives since childhood.

I was an English major and studied Shakespeare at depth. Years later I came to recognize how so many of the Bard's great truths applied to my life. For instance, Shakespeare tells us that the world is a stage and each of us is playing a part, a role. Our lines are scripted, and although we have a certain amount of control over our part, ultimately our influence is limited.

The wise person who is able to witness the play, to stand back and watch what is unfolding without becoming attached to certain outcomes, is AWAKE. Like Jesus, the awake person is *in this world but not of it*. While she is a participant, she operates by conscious choice, rather than running on auto-pilot as most of us do. Those who don't question or remain objective in life respond to the world based on unconscious beliefs, rules, fears, and limitations. The awakened individual consciously evaluates what is happening and instinctively knows what to do and how to respond in order to gain the best possible outcome for self and others. As the witness, we can watch ourselves playing our part and remain calm and detached amid the most horrific situations we may encounter. At times we will become upset or have some other reaction that is part of our being human. But underneath whatever is happening we will maintain a peace of mind and know that chaos, pain, and change are simply parts of our process.

As we become aware, remember, that we can consciously choose the meaning and value of our experiences – that we in fact CREATE OUR OWN REALITY. We learn to make wise choices rather than relying on our society, our families, or our cultures to choose meanings and responses for us. In the auto-pilot mode so many of us choose, we spend a lot of time in pain and suffering and, as someone once said, our creativity remains stillborn. We are all influenced by outside forces; but when we learn to operate independent of them, understanding our inherent power of choice, we can improve upon any situation and create a different story. As long as we remain passive, not consciously choosing the way we respond to life, we remain helpless victims. Operating independently and from an awakened consciousness, we will choose ways to navigate this lifetime that bring us peace and happiness. That's when we realize that we're not here to CONTROL what happens, but rather to respond to what is in the highest and best way possible.

Because the meanings we give things have consequences, we need to choose wisely. Mindful that everything is neutral until WE assign it a value, that nothing has intrinsic worth, learn to choose what will bring happiness and a sense of well-being and contentment. Taking the high road, we learn to view life, to witness what goes on around us, from a high spot on the mountain rather than down in the valley where so many of us spend our lives.

Consider all the filters that cause us to judge things and people as we do: our memories, our beliefs, our values, the strategies we employ – all input from our environment. When these filters and their results are unconscious, life just "happens" to us and often feels beyond our control. When we employ a conscious filtering process, we exercise choices and create the outcomes we desire. Unfortunately most of us get stuck in patterns, habits, built around pain and insecurity, desperate attempts to remain safe by avoiding change. Ironically, we can become attached to the issues that frighten us most.

Take worry, for instance. My dad use to tell us that worrying is nothing but a waste of time and energy: what will be will be. Well part of that advice is worth taking; but the "what will be" part, now *that* I can change. And I can change what might be an undesirable outcome by CHOOSING to respond differently to whatever is up. For instance, perhaps something frightening has entered our life, such as a terminal diagnosis for ourselves or a loved one. Now imagine the worst possible outcome: I may die. Reconcile yourself that death may in fact occur. After all, sooner or later it will come to us all. Maybe the doctor IS right; but then again, maybe not! Get busy doing everything you can to prove the diagnosis wrong. That way, regardless of the outcome, you will experience the best you can with whatever time remains.

Have you ever known someone who, near death, seems to have found peace, a beautiful acceptance that change awaits them? Once we reconcile ourselves to the "worst" possible outcome, nothing can disturb the peace of mind we can embrace. And is it possible – just possible – that death, like sickness, doesn't deserve the negative rap we've all given it for seemingly ever? After all, death and sickness are neutral occurrences until we assign them a value. The truth is both are parts of our human existence, things we will all experience at one time or another. Is it possible, absent a terminal diagnosis, to be at peace – now, when you're in good health – with this notion of death, to redefine the meaning it has held for eons?

The wonderful thing about CHANGE is that we're inviting our lives to expand for the better. When I was in the throes of the deep depression that led to thoughts of suicide and hospitalization, it truly felt as if my world was falling apart – and that I had no control over my circumstances. But of course I did; and the fact that I CHOSE to self-admit to a psychiatric facility when I did – going against my doctor's advice – demonstrated that truth. Detox was a horrible experience, but I obviously survived, in fact thrived in the end. I now look back on how with each and every successive trial I've faced – whether another bout of depression (which thankfully I haven't had for over seven years now) or anything else the world labels "bad" – the time I've spent with the pain has not only been significantly shorter, it has been easier for me to negotiate. And that's largely due to the fact that I've surrendered to the situation, not attached myself to the need for a particular outcome, and have trusted the Universe to its divine timing, recognizing that, once again, I'm being invited to grow!

The more awake, the more conscious, I become, the more intentional rather than reactive I am. If I find myself suffering, I realize I am choosing to feel bad, that I can stop feeling that way – stop resisting what is – and just be okay. The immediate shift in my experience is dramatic. Maybe I choose, consciously, to feel sad over a loved one's death and how meaningful that loss is. And that's fine, as it should be. But when I choose to realize that my life has now changed in some way, because that individual is no longer in it, I can allow a new beginning to take shape, knowing both of us are now free to move on. I can choose to fill the void with loving memories, even as I move on to create new ones.

I recently took part in a memorial celebration that was so filled with energy and love that all who participated felt uplifted by having attended. Tears were shed, but laughter was shared as well. And music, a lot of music, as this dear one was a musician of note. The entire service was about giving thanks for all the incredible gifts our friend had shared. And we all recognized that although his physical presence was no more, his loving energy and enormous contributions would live on with us forever.

4

CAUSE AND THE WITNESS

■ ■ ■

The most fundamental law of life is the law of cause and effect. When we live in an unconscious, reactive way, present relationships and experiences can activate, or trigger, old wounds. When that happens we are "at effect" rather than at cause. Without intending to, we can perpetuate dysfunctional behaviors and beliefs; and it takes very little reinforcement for reactive behavior to become habitual.

The witness, as noted earlier, is that part of us that observes what is happening as it occurs. It's as though you're standing outside yourself and observing what you're doing and how you're feeling. While the witness just watches, in unconscious reactor mode knee-jerk reactions take hold of us.

Have you ever noticed how hardly a second passes when you're not judging something or someone? It might be as simple as how the room temperature feels, or as damaging as believing the person sitting next to you on the bus is your enemy. Years ago I became aware of the difference between "judging" and "discerning." While the former places value on something or someone, the latter is merely making note of what is occurring, without condemnation or praise. The witness with the discerning eye sees events and people without labeling or valuing them. The witness perspective is the healthy one, and we play that role when we consciously choose the meaning of what's happening in our life and world. In that way we become both author and witness to what occurs. And whatever happens is okay. Yet in this role of observer we can note things we want to do differently, things that will make a positive difference for us and for others.

As witness we view life with curiosity rather than judgment. As witness we go with the flow, no resistance. And with no resistance, we don't suffer. What this all boils down to is simply this: without resistance we don't suffer. And as the observer or witness, we create peace and happiness. Curiosity is a wonderful panacea for what ails us, what makes us feel misery and pain. When you watch what happens when you suffer (for instance, what happens to your body and peace of mind when you're angry), the suffering goes away. Curiosity leads to detachment, and then you recognize you're free to choose. You are at cause when you CHOOSE happiness, not when you wait, victimized, for happiness to come to you. You create the life you wish to live.

The challenge in moving toward a life as witness is that part of us (ego) resists change and wants to hang on to old beliefs out of a false sense of security. Uncovering beliefs that no longer serve us is a life-long process. So many beliefs that operate at an unconscious level result from our upbringing and societal influences. The question to ask is not whether they're good or bad, but whether they serve you in a positive way. If a belief or action leads to greater peace and happiness, it's serving you well. If not, you're better off changing some way of viewing or operating in this world. The witness serves you well. And the more you pay attention as an "outsider" to your words, feelings, and actions, the sooner you will experience more happiness. Ultimately, happiness will be your state of being: it will occur spontaneously. But that takes time and practice. And there's no better time to begin than right now! When you choose to be AT CAUSE rather than the passive EFFECT of life happening TO you, you take responsibility for your life, you own your power (which is unlimited), and you know how it feels to be free and whole as the unique and perfect expression of God that you are.

5

WHEN A SHIFT HAPPENS

■ ■ ■

First of all, what do I mean by the word "shift?" As the name implies, a shift is movement, and in the sense I use it, it's an upward movement. A positive expression of growth. While it may be dramatic – noticeable as was Paul's experience on the road to Damascus – more likely it will be subtle, occurring over time. But in either event, it will be positive, life-enhancing.

However a shift is experienced, when it occurs we awaken in some manner, noticing and sensing Life in a deeper and grander way than we previously could have imagined. In order for shifts to occur, we must be ready and willing to give up some old way of being as shifts imply change. When a shift occurs in your life, it may seem as though the entire world, at least your personal relationships, have changed for the better. Usually those changes have not occurred, but because **your perspective has changed**, you see others and your world differently.

A shift invites and allows you to see things from that witness point of view – that is, things seem to be happening just as they should be. Rather than judging, you now experience life with compassion and non-attachment. From a bit of positive distance you become more effective and responsive, rather than fearful and reactive.

As each of us grows in acceptance of ourselves and others, we become better able to handle stress and no longer become caught up in everyday traumas that continue to occur. We no longer need to feel in a hurry, knowing there is enough time for everything. Instead of feeling stressed, we now feel curiosity, interest, and confidence. We KNOW that life is unfolding in the right and perfect way, for everyone involved. We are able to get out of the way and just let life happen!

When we can view our world from the mountaintop rather than the valley, we are better able (more energized and inspired) to do our work, to seek desirable outcomes, and yet remain unattached to what happens. We CARE, but we don't suffer. That's how compassion feels. We have preferences, but now we discern rather than judge. As the witness you have become, now you operate in the world as "an antidote to the poison of resistance" and its attendant suffering. Remember that without resistance there is no suffering.

It's exciting to realize that you're growing, but as I've said before, it's not particularly easy. As science and history have demonstrated time and time again, chaos is essential for growth to occur. When we learn to welcome the disruptions and disturbances that accompany change, we remember that death to old ways of being means new, higher ways are being birthed. And more times than not, shifts occur as the result of changes over time or, as I've said about the process before, we grow in baby steps more often than in quantum leaps. But when we're ready for a leap, it will occur in such a way that we are prepared to do whatever it takes, recognizing that a positive transformation is taking place. An experience we would have found overwhelming at an earlier time, we can now welcome with curiosity and excitement.

For me the most exciting process of growth is recognizing that I am the one in charge of my life, that I am a powerful instrument for change, not only my own, but even change in the world around me. The more I take responsibility for what occurs, the happier and more peaceful my life becomes. Life happens outside of me, of course, but I now respond to what happens in a different, more positive, more powerful way. I am awake and conscious of my choices. Unlike the feeling of victimhood, which is what I experience when I am the EFFECT of what happens TO me, I have become the CAUSE, responsible for everything that happens, for the way I feel and my behavior. Now rather than playing a role in a drama, I am the star of a light-hearted, entertaining production that is guaranteed to have a happy outcome.

I no longer operate in auto-pilot mode. Now as I observe what is happening around me and choose how I respond to it, I am conscious. And when fully conscious, in a split second I can process all possible outcomes and select the one that serves me best. Examine your life today, pay attention to how you respond – or react – to events around you. Do you behave like Pavlov's dog, instantly salivating when it hears the dinner bell? Do feelings of anxiety provoke reactions of anger or fear, make you want to tense up, run away, talk excitedly, drink, or in some other way distract yourself from a situation that is uncomfortable? Is drama, unhappiness, or worry the result? If so, you're operating on auto-pilot, responding unconsciously to a situation based on rules, regulations, or beliefs you learned early in life that no longer serve you.

Perhaps the greatest benefit you gain when you awaken and live consciously is that it becomes impossible for you to do anything that isn't in your best interests. If you start to do something that is in some way destructive, your conscious awareness causes it – a belief, a value, a feeling, or a behavior – to disappear; you simply cannot do something that isn't good for you when you are conscious!

Remember how you learned to ride a bike, or tie your shoes. You practiced; you got it wrong more often than not. UNTIL one day you got it right! And from that day on it was a proverbial piece of cake. And so it is with becoming conscious, of awakening to life with all its magnificent potential. You'll make mistakes; but every time you get back on the bike – move into the role of the non-resistant witness – and keep going, keep trying, at some point you'll be living a conscious life and it will make all the difference. Until that day, be vigilant, stay committed, and recognize your habitual ways of going unconscious. All without judgment. If you get angry, stop: how do you feel; what old messages got triggered? Become curious about your own ways of living, and remain detached from the outcome. Certainly you can PREFER a particular outcome, but as long as you remain detached from it, you'll always feel okay. Your life, your feelings, won't depend on what happens around you.

The past does not have to be prologue. But for many of us, it is. Those are the folks who live their lives on auto-pilot, never questioning the source of their beliefs, their values, their judgments of right and wrong, good and bad. Questioning does not necessarily lead to a change of habit. Questioning simply informs us whether something benefits us, or is no longer of value. Part of our work as evolving souls is to examine our most deeply held beliefs, beliefs about ourselves and about our world. As you do this work – and I encourage you to write down your discoveries – look at what is happening in your life right now. You will notice that what you're attracting (opportunities, money, love) directly reflects your core beliefs. Do you feel really good about yourself? If you do, your life will mirror those positive feelings and you'll prosper in all ways. If there are areas where you'd like to manifest something different, what's the old, habitual message you're telling yourself that you need to work at changing?

None of these practices involves blame. Those people or influences that created our beliefs at a very young and vulnerable age (we were vulnerable because we simply didn't know better) weren't "bad," or "ignorant," or intentionally "hurtful." If their beliefs didn't serve them well, they simply hadn't yet awakened. It's never too late to create new beliefs and habits. Focus on what you want. Before you go to sleep and when you first wake up, focus on how you want your day to be. You're writing a new script for your life and you'll be memorizing new lines as it were. That takes time and practice, dedication to perfecting your new role as a resourceful and powerful influence for good in this world. Affirm and embrace your power, power that enables you to create the life you want.

As T.S. Eliot wrote in the **Four Quartets**, "*What we most desire is already within us. Our job is to be quiet and wait.*" I would add that as we spend time in the silence, affirming our new beliefs, we also take time to move our feet in the direction we want to go, the direction we want our life to go. And do so without resistance to whatever may show up in the process. It's all good!

6

ACCESSING A HIGHER CONSCIOUSNESS

■ ■ ■

While conscious living doesn't have to wait until we start conscious aging, in my case the years of my life now past have definitely served me well as I move through what I think of as stage two of midlife adulthood. This stage of life isn't about glorifying youth or denying aging or mortality. Rather, for me it's about valuing the aging process.

The only birthday I remember ever dreading was my fiftieth. And yet when that day finally rolled around, it was the most liberating, exhilarating birthday I'd ever had. Why had I dreaded it so? Now at "midlife" I was free to do anything, say anything, be anyone I wanted; I'd earned the right. And it was also a turning point in the receiving/ giving roles we often play. Now started my time of life to give back, to mentor others as I had been mentored myself.

To paraphrase psychologist and preeminent researcher of the human psyche, Carl Jung, we can't live the afternoon of our lives the way we lived the mornings; the program that was great when it worked in the mornings will be of little use come evening. And what was true in the morning will be a lie in the evening. And while I personally don't care for the term "elder," I respect its meaning. I, and others my age or there-abouts, have earned the recognition and respect we hopefully receive as we move into and through this period of mentoring the "morning folks."

When asked what consciousness means to me, I explain that it means becoming aware of who I am at the most authentic, highest level of my Being. This state of Self-awareness comes as a result of being open to and curious about the infinite ways in which the Life Force I call God expresses; learning to discern rather than judge; and recognizing the many ways we are both diverse as unique beings, and one and the same as a result of our core essence. That core essence, of course, is the Creative Energy of Love (or God), First Cause of all there is, has ever been, and will ever be.

Unfortunately this planet we inhabit is shrouded in a very dark cloud of unconsciousness. Those operating on auto-pilot and not questioning why they do what they do still outnumber those of us who have opened to another way of viewing our world, our lives, and our interdependence. As we know, however, the slightest bit of light dispels the darkness; so as our unifying and growing collective light grows, we will survive and overcome to redefine the role of elder as it has previously been known.

And it certainly doesn't take growing into this wonderful time of second midlife adulthood to become conscious. In the past fifty or more years babies have entered this lifetime with amazing telepathic and psychic abilities. We're seeing an increase in intuitive, creative, and abstract thinking abilities, along with increased instances of ADHD, autism, and dyslexia. All these incredible talents signal evolutionary changes that are at work in the collective human consciousness.

For most of us, however, bringing forth gifts and talents from past lives, and developing new skills that help us understand and advance our awareness, takes time, practice, patience, and perseverance. Growing with intention is key to positive living and positive aging.

Whatever I write and whenever I speak my core message is always the same: we are each unique and profoundly spiritual beings, some more aware of this Truth than others, but all on the same journey that is the process of enlightenment. As we work to deepen conscious awareness of our inherent spiritual dimension, we are able to transform once disempowering stories into powerful new ways of understanding the challenges and hardships we've faced. In this process of turning pain to gain, our perspective shifts from that of a limited ego's view – that difficult, painful experiences are many and to be avoided – to a more inclusive view that is vaster, wiser, and more acute. This is our soul's perspective that informs us that our life's purpose includes a destiny that will unfold through unique experiences, both pleasant and painful. In each and every circumstance and relationship, we can choose to learn and grow into the people we have the divine potential to become. We can achieve this high purpose through a high level of consciousness we call Self-awareness.

From this broader perspective we can appreciate that past wounds and traumas have taught us about compassion and empathy, resilience and the importance of appropriate boundaries. Perhaps we lost a job we loved so we would be pushed into a challenging search that would result in a fuller expression of our gifts. Ultimately our most difficult and painful times have allowed, maybe even forced, us to see the limits of our egos as we turned inward to our spiritual depths for guidance. Pain is part of our human story. But how we interpret our painful times and the stories we create around them can empower rather than disempower us, teaching us about the behaviors and attitudes that don't serve us as well as those that do. As we become able to relate to our most difficult times as agents for our growth, we free up positive energy for the work we have left to do in this lifetime.

CONCLUSION

■ ■ ■

My goal in writing this book has been to share with you suggestions, ideas, and experiences that will help you recover from losses and live a happy life, whatever circumstances you may face. The only question you ever need to ask and answer is this simple one: ***Do I want to be happy?*** If your answer is YES, you need to let any deep-seated preferences not get in your way. Your happiness is under your control, but in order to be happy you mustn't qualify your YES with a "but," "when," or "if." Your YES must be unconditional!

Unconditional happiness is the best path toward enlightenment, which, of course, is yet another process. Be advised, however, that once you decide to choose unconditional happiness as your path, something will inevitably challenge you. It will test your commitment, and whatever the problem may be, you mustn't let it bother you. Don't let other people's behavior jolt you off your path.

Spiritual work is all about learning to live free of worry, fear, and melodrama. Stress only occurs when you're resisting the way life is. When you really think about resistance, like worry, it never does any good. When we resist, something – that which we resist – has already happened. So you can't change reality. Your resistance is the experience of some event passing through us. It's a total waste of your energy. If you're a chronic resister, over time energies will build up to the point that you will be so blocked you'll either blow up or shut down completely. I was very near that point when I was hospitalized. It's never life's events that cause our problem, but our resistance to them.

Based on previous experiences and our beliefs, we all carry around our set of preconceived notions about how things should be. History implants impressions in our mind, and when something triggers an unhappy memory, we resist. The better approach is to move into that witness or observer role and ask yourself why, whatever it is, is that bothering you. Remember that when you're curious, you move into a neutral gear and can evaluate your situation objectively. Events are just events; your resistance to them causes the problems. As Don Miguel Ruiz says in *The Four Agreements*, don't take it personally.

Our fears and desires, born of something in our past, are the feelings that cause resistance to enter the picture. As I've explored in my earlier books, relationships are a great way to work on yourself. The path to making relationships work and prosper is to not try and make people fit into your preconceived molds of how they should be. The same goes for your work, whatever it is you do. Work should be fun. When we're content to deal only with what we face at any moment, we won't be worrying about anything. More love moves through and around us as energy that we once bottled up is freed up to move and flow. And that's what it means to live life fully!

POST-SCRIPT

■ ■ ■

This book, unlike most, calls for a "PS," or post-script. As mentioned early on, Mr. R and I broke up over the Christmas holidays. After spending almost a month apart, we decided to re-group.

During our time apart, and particularly on the holidays themselves, I made great efforts, most successful, to stay busy with friends and activities. Christmas Day my son and his pup joined me and my pup for a low-keyed holiday meal. Originally my brother, his son and partner, and possibly her aunt, were going to join us from out of town. At the last minute those plans morphed, so it ended up just the two of us and another eight legs.

Once alone later Christmas night, and feeling a bit down, I stretched out to watch a little mindless television. I heard my cell text ring, alerting me that someone was trying to contact me. When I looked at the message, I didn't recognize the area code or number, and no name was given. The text simply said, "Marry Christmas, Susan." I found out that the area code was Portland, Oregon and I couldn't recall knowing anyone from that city. Curious, I texted back, "Who wants me to 'marry' Christmas?" I expected the "a" was just a typo, intended as an "e," but I decided to have some fun.

The return text, beginning "See if you remember these," continued with a string of emails this man and I had exchanged almost a year earlier. It turned out that although I was already in a committed relationship at that time, we met for coffee just in case....Because I knew my then current partner and I were limited in how far we could go (due to significant philosophical differences), I'd kept my on-line MATCH account active; and from time to time either I would reach out of someone would contact me. This particular man, with whom I had a lengthy phone conversation before meeting, was indeed an interesting person.

Back to Christmas night. We texted a bit more and made another coffee date for two weeks later, as he was traveling over the New Year's holiday. That encounter lifted my spirits. And although I had sworn off looking for *yet another man*, this one had reached out to me and with one face-to-face meeting behind us, I knew I'd enjoy getting to learn more about him.

The next day I called my brother and decided I'd visit him over the year-end holiday. I did and ended up spending an enjoyable week out of town. It was just what my internal doctor prescribed, and I felt much better upon returning to Atlanta. During the time since I'd last seen Mr. R I'd come to a number of realizations.

The tears I'd shed early on right after our splitting, had been mostly about my feeling sad for Mr. R. It was interesting that I didn't feel sorry for myself or for our decision to end the relationship. That in itself felt like progress to me. As I spent time in the quiet those first few days, I became increasingly clear that everything in my life was ABSOLUTELY okay, even good. While he and I had come together to resolve some karma from a much earlier time, we both agreed we'd missed the boat on accomplishing that end, and we would just have to trust the Universe, because It clearly knew better than we about how and what needed healing in our relationship.

While I had no intention of contacting Mr. R, I also told myself that if he reached out and wanted to talk, I was perfectly fine doing that. I'd come to the conclusion that if we were done, we were done; or, if we agreed to try again, that would be fine as well. We met, we talked at length, and we decided to try again. And this time it would be a day to day experience, with few if any expectations. Another significant change in the way I'd always operated. Clearly my need to control the situation had disappeared. We both recognized and agreed about what had gone awry with our communication issues. It was obvious to me, very quickly, that Mr. R was making a conscious effort to keep his temper under control and exercise patience, when in the past we would have bumped heads. He acknowledged the same in regard to my behavior. Maybe, just maybe, we'd learned enough about each other and ourselves that this time we could make a successful go of our relationship.

As I conclude this book, we're still living together, allowing each other more latitude than was previously the case, and enjoying the time we do spend together. As for the future, what will be, will be. Ours now is very much a one-day-at-a-time approach to this relationship. No attachment to any particular outcome, and no resistance.... All is well. I'm at peace with Susan and loving who I AM. And I know that as I continue to consciously release old habits and attitudes that no longer serve me, those feelings of contentment will only increase. After all, we manifest what we practice!

References

The Essential Rumi: New Expanded Addition (translation by Coleman Barks). HarperCollins 2004.

Brumet, Robert. *Finding Yourself in Transition*, Unity Books 2001.

Butterworth, Eric. *Discover the Power Within You*, Harper & Row 1989.

Chapman, Gary. *The 5 Love Languages*, Northfield Publishing 2015.

Chodran, Pima. *When Things Fall Apart*, Shambala 2000.

Gibran, Kahlil. *The Prophet*, Alfred Knopf 1989.

James, William. *Varieties of Religious Experience*, Random House 1994.

Ruiz, Don Miguel. *The Four Agreements*, Amber-Allen Publishing 1997.

Trammell, Susan Truett. *Outrageous Loving!* Self-Published 2015.

_. *The Sacred Alchemy of Love*, Self-Published 2014.

Made in the USA
San Bernardino, CA
23 July 2018